Kersey Graves, John T Perry

Sixteen Saviours or One? T

Vol. 1

Kersey Graves, John T Perry
Sixteen Saviours or One? T
Vol. 1

ISBN/EAN: 9783337314415

Printed in Europe, USA, Canada, Australia, Japan

Cover: Foto ©Lupo / pixelio.de

More available books at **www.hansebooks.com**

Sixteen Saviours or One?

THE GOSPELS NOT BRAHMANIC.

—BY—

JOHN T. PERRY.

"We are no Brachmans, or Indian Gymnosophists, dwellers in woods remote from the affairs of life. We know that our duty is to give thanks to God, the Lord and the Creator."—*Tertullian.*

CINCINNATI:
PETER G. THOMSON, 179 Vine Street.
1879.

To my Father:

Who, at the age of more than ninety years, still retains his interest in the great questions which bear upon man's nature and destiny; This volume is affectionately and gratefully inscribed.

INTRODUCTION.

OF making of books there is no end, and every addition to the already overgrown mass of literature should have ample justification. This little volume claims no exemption from the responsibility because of its diminutive size, but trusts that its subject and purpose will sufficiently excuse its appearance.

The skepticism prevalent among well-read people, may be as hostile to revelation as the infidelity of eighty or one hundred years ago, but it is more decorous. It alleges historical criticism and scientific discovery as the bases of its conclusions, and rarely gets into a passion. Yet the iconoclastic school of Paine and Voltaire is not dead. It has only found new pupils. The earliest opponents of the Bible, though radicals in theory, were aristocrats in practice. Anthony Collins, perhaps the ablest of the English deists of the first half of the last century, always sent his servants to church, that they might not rob him. Voltaire denounced with severity Holbach's "Good Sense," because it taught atheism to valets and chambermaids. It was not until Paine, a man of the people, wrote in a strictly popular manner, that the English masses were provided with a scheme of unbelief suited to their tastes and comprehension.

During the quarter of a century following our Revolution, the influence of the "Age of Reason" was paramount among the radical democracy of New York. Dr. John W. Francis has given in his "Old New York" a fearful picture of the demoralization of the period. Elihu Palmer, a blind man and apostate minister, lectured regularly to a chosen circle, by which he was regarded as infallible, and second only to the great Thomas. In his "Principles of Nature" he has left behind him a summary of his deistical scheme.

Thirty years later, the lectures of Frances Wright and Robert Dale Owen, and their paper, the *Free Enquirer*, spread atheism among the working people of New York. Benjamin Offen, a "philosophical" shoemaker, also lectured at Tammany Hall. The late Gilbert Vale united the callings of a mathemetical instrument maker and publisher of skeptical works, and about the same time Abner Kneeland started the *Investigator* at Boston. "Liberal" papers were also established in other places, but they all, and the *Enquirer* as well, soon died out. The movement seemed to have culminated. The *Investigator* alone maintained a somewhat sickly existence, and its publisher issued a list of skeptical works at very high prices. Judging from the persistency with which old editions were kept on sale the demand was not very large.

Recently a change for the worse has taken place. Infidel Spiritualism has allied itself to out-and-out materialism, and its advocates are pushing the same books and manifesting entire sympathy in the anti-christian warfare of the successors of Kneeland. There are now at least three houses in New York, two in Boston and one in Chicago, which publish long lists of books and tracts assailing the Christian faith, the divine existence, and often the sanctity of marriage. Some of these publications have passed through numerous editions, and all are thoroughly adapted to shake the belief of those who are unfamiliar with the questions discussed. Their authors are either persons, who having no reputation to lose, are utterly unscrupulous in their statements, or men who, having prejudged the case, are incapable of fairly weighing evidence. Anything that will serve their purpose in telling against Christianity is good enough for them. Writing in this spirit, it is not strange that their productions should appear very weighty to the unsophisticated. They never fail to make out a "good case."

The great majority of these effusions are not read by what is known as the reading public, and many of their special objections and assertions are not noticed in the standard volumes on the evidences of Christianity. For about fifty years Robert Taylor's Diegesis has been published in Boston with the advertisement that it is deemed "unanswerable in fact and argument," yet it has received little attention. The Rev. George E. Ellis reviewed it in *The Christian Examiner* over forty years ago. The paper is excellent as far as it goes, but hardly sufficient as an answer to a work, very dangerous, because extremely dishonest, and so besprinkled with Greek and Hebrew as to wear the appearance of profound scholarship. It will not do to say that noticing books of this kind serves to advertise them. They are already advertised, and are sowing the seeds of unbelief, communism and recklessness of all kinds among large numbers of voters. If clergymen and philanthropists wish to know all the reasons for non-attendance at church among the working classes, they will do well to inquire into the circulation of books and pamphlets unknown to them, yet filled with deadly poison.

Some time ago my attention was called to the works of Mr. Kersey Graves, a skeptical spiritualist of Richmond, Indiana. I first heard of their wide circulation at the East. As they had passed through several editions, I did not feel that I ran any risk of giving them undue publicity by commenting upon them. It seemed best to make my strictures known in the author's own locality. My friend Mr. Daniel Surface of the *Richmond Telegram*, kindly gave me ample space in his columns, and I reviewed at length the two volumes of Mr. Graves which have gained the widest circulation.

He replied, and I rejoined. The controversy then closed, not because Mr. Graves had no desire to prolong it, but because the publisher of the *Telegram* thought the subject had been exhausted. The three articles make up this volume. The public care of course very little about Mr. Graves and myself, but I have chosen to reproduce the discussion, with no changes save the correction of typographical errors, the amendment of a few hastily written sentences, and the addition of a note or two, in my own letters. I have made no alteration in Mr. Graves', defense, but have inserted two or three shcrt communications in which he corrected or explained what he had said before. The reader will thus be able to see what each side has to urge for itself. It is not as a discussion however, that I ask attention to the book. I think I can claim first, that the main arguments of Taylor's Diegesis, Volney's Ruins, Higgins' Anacalypsis, and Jacolliot's Bible in India, as well as those of Mr. Graves himself, are fully and fairly met; second, that the materials here gathered must be sought elsewhere in more than one authority and are not to be found in the ordinarily accessible defenses of the Bible. The positions refuted are those which compose the stronghold of the infidel working-men throughout the country, and hence deserve the special attention of the clergy. Furthermore, some of them are gaining a revived acceptance among writers of more eminence than the last named, and a new edition of the Anacalypsis, which has long been out of print, is announced.

I make no pretensions to scholarship; I have simply endeavored to study my subject carefully and thoroughly, and honestly to record my conclusions. The field of comparative mythology is a vast one, and no single person can hope to view, much less to till its entire surface. I have been compelled through lack of space to confine myself to one or two vital issues. If I have shown that Christ is no copy of Krishna, and Christianity no modification of any of the old ethnic beliefs, I have not been unconscious of the many curious ramifications, survivals of a primitive revelation, or proofs of the spiritual unity of all men—which unite the faiths of widely separated nations. I have glanced at these in passing, but they are much more satisfactorily, though briefly, set forth in a note from Professor Swing, which will be found in the appendix. My authorities are sufficiently credited in the context. I wish, however, to acknowledge special obligations to Hardwick's "Christ and other Masters," a work remarkable for its keen analysis of the differences as well as resemblances between Christianity and the ethnic faiths. Cardinal Wiseman's "Lectures on the Connection between Science and Revealed Religion," are also no less valuable in regard to certain essential points, because some of their statements respecting natural science have become antiquated during the more than forty years, which have elapsed since their delivery.

No one can be more conscious of the defects of my work than myself. I could plead in extenuation the unceasing demands of a daily newspaper, yet I have yielded to the request of many friends and readers that I should incorporate my articles in a permanent form. I hope their expectations and my desire of the good thus to be attained will not be disappointed.

GAZETTE OFFICE.   J. T. P.

Cincinnati, April 15, 1879.

"The Sixteen Crucified Saviors."

Mr. KERSEY GRAVES AS A THEOLOGIAN AND SCHOLAR.

To the Editor of the Richmond Telegram:

INTRODUCTORY.

The controversy on the evidences of Christianity has assumed various forms. Sometimes one position has been assailed by skeptics, and sometimes another. Each campaign has had its peculiar tactics. While borrowing from those which preceded it whatever seemed serviceable, those weapons that had proved valueless were thrown away. Just now German rationalists and their English and American imitators are chiefly anxious to prove that the Old and New Testament records are not the work of their reputed authors, but of a sufficiently later origin to allow time for mythical and legendary narratives to grow up. There are others who place their reliance on the alleged discrepancies of revelation and science, forgetting that natural philosophers have changed ground in hundreds of particulars within the last quarter of a century, and that the shifting process has by no means ceased.

The people of Richmond are pretty generally aware, I suppose, that their fellow citizen, Mr. Kersey Graves, published a few years ago a volume with the surprising title of "THE WORLD'S SIXTEEN CRUCIFIED SAVIORS, OR CHRISTIANITY BEFORE CHRIST," of which the fourth edition now lies before me. It purports to contain, "new, startling, and extraordinary revelations in religious history, which disclose the oriental origin of all the doctrines, principles, precepts and miracles of the Christian New Testament, and furnishing a key for unlocking many of its sacred mysteries, besides comprising the history of sixteen heathen crucified gods." In an "Address to the Clergy," prefixed to the main work, he informs the teachers of the Christian faith that "The divine claims of your (their) religion are gone—all swept away by the 'logic of history,' and nullified by the demonstrations of science." He then repeats in detail various alleged coincidences between the scriptural records of the birth, life, and death of Christ and the so-called saviours, who, he says, preceded Him; the inference, of course, being that the claims of all are equally true and equally false, since the "primary constituent elements and properties of human nature being essentially the same in all countries, and all centuries, and the feeling called Religion being a spontaneous outgrowth of the human mind, the coincidence would naturally produce similar feelings, similar thoughts," &c. He further says:

"Researches into oriental history reveal the remarkable fact that the stories of incarnate Gods answering to and resembling the miraculous character of Jesus Christ have been prevalent in most, if not all, the principal religious heathen nations of antiquity; (were there any irreligious ones?) and the accounts and narratives of some of these deific incarnations bear such a striking example to that of the Christian Savior—not only in their general features, but in some cases in the most minute details, from the legend of the immaculate conception, to that of the crucifixion, and subsequent ascension into heaven—that one might almost be mistaken for the other."

If he has demonstrated, as he claims to have done, the foregoing positions, any further assault on Christianity would be very much like kicking a corpse, yet we fancy that Mr. Graves is not quite as confident, on sober second thought, as he was while the glow of authorship was fresh, for he has just favored the public with a second effusion of the same general character, and involving, we must say, quite a number of repetitions. The new volume is styled, "THE BIBLE OF BIBLES, OR TWENTY-SEVEN DIVINE REVELATIONS," containing a description of twenty-seven Bibles, and an exposition (we suppose he means exposure) of two thousand biblical errors in Science, History, Morals, Religion and General Events; also, a delineation of the character of the principal personages of the Christian Bible, and an examination of their doctrines."

The first of the two books is the more important, but a review of its contents will involve an inquiry into the antiquity and merits of the chief heathen "bibles," while the author's estimate of the character and evidences of the Hebrew and Christian scriptures, being the same in both volumes, may be considered without exclusive reference to either.

Before beginning on the "Sixteen Saviors," Mr. Graves names

thirty-five persons, historical and mythological, who have received or claimed divine honors. Among these are Salivahana, of *Bermuda!* Though the word we have italicized is twice repeated, we will hold the proof reader responsible for relegating an East Indian divinity to the new world. Mohammed is also in the list, though he never pretended to be more than a prophet. Ixion is set down by Mr. Graves as a Roman, though he appears in the classics as a fabulous king of Thessaly, who was tied to a wheel in Hades for being too intimate with Juno. As he was a murderer before he became a libertine in the circles of Olympus he is certainly a queer candidate for supernatural dignity.

THE SIXTEEN "SAVIORS."

But we will pass to the sixteen who, our author asserts, were believed to have been crucified in or about the years affixed to their names. They are Chrishna, of India, 1200 B. C.; the Hindoo Sakia, 600 B. C.; Thammuz, of Syria, 1160 B. C.; Wittoba, of the Telengonese, 552 B. C.; Iao, of Nepaul, 622 B. C.; Hesus, of the Celtic Druids, 834 B. C.; Quexalcote, of Mexico, 587 B. C.; Quirinus, of Rome, 506 B. C.; (Aeschylus) Prometheus, crucified 547 B. C.; Thulis, of Egypt, 1700 B. C.; Indra of Thibet, 725 B. C.; Alcestos (we suppose Alcestis is meant), of Euripides, 600 B. C.; Atys, of Phrygia, 1170 B. C.; Crite, of Chaldea, 200 B. C.; Bali, of Orissa, 725 B. C.; Mithra, of Persia, 600 B. C.

After reading the astounding catalogue, the reader will naturally inquire whether the statements are true? We are afraid we shall have to reduce the list very materially before we consider certain theories not original with Mr. Graves, upon which all his conclusions are based. Sakia, who is no other than Buddha, must first be dismissed. He is a historical character, a reformer and founder of an important sect. He never was crucified, however, but died a natural death at the age of about eighty, four hundred years or more before Christ. The earliest canon of his writings was not formed until a century and a half after his death. None of the miraculous stories concerning his birth can be traced back to a period preceding the Christian era. The oldest writings concerning him extant—there are two sets, the southern and northern, of which the latter are the more marvelous—are subsequent to the Christian era, in their present form at least.

Thammuz, or the Tammuz, is an Eastern version of the mythical Greek character Adonis, the beloved of Venus, who was killed by a boar, not by crucifixion.

Hesus, sometimes called Esus, not Eros, the god of love, as Mr. Graves prints it, was the Celtic war god, the counterpart of the Roman Mars, and, as some affirm, the chief divinity, whose symbol was the oak.

Quexalcote, or Quetzalcoatl, as Prescott spells his name, was the Mexican god of the air. During his residence on earth, it is said, he instructed the natives in the use of metals, in agriculture, and in the arts of government. From some cause, not explained, the historian of the Conquest of Mexico, tells us "Quetzalcoatl incurred the wrath of one of the principal gods and was compelled to abandon the country. On his way he stopped at the city of Cholula, where a temple was dedicated to his worship, the mossy ruins of which still form one of the most interesting relics of antiquity in Mexico. When he reached the shores of the Mexican gulf, he took leave of his followers, promising that he and his descendants would revisit them hereafter, and then entering his wizard skiff, made of serpents' skins, embarked on the great ocean for the fabled land of Tlapallan."

Quirinus, of Rome, is only our old friend Romulus, under the title given him on his deification after his mysterious disappearance. The name also belongs to Mars, his reputed father. He was no more a savior than any of the later Roman emperors who arrogated to themselves divine honors.

As for Thulis, or Zulis, of Egypt, whom Mr. Graves makes a saviour about the time that Jacob was serving Laban, we are told that he was the same as Apis, the sacred bull of Memphis, who was sacrificed if he reached the age of twenty-five years, though it was pretended that he drowned himself. This animal could hardly be called a crucified saviour, though he was supposed to be glorified by the indwelling of Osiris. The biggest bull, however, in the case, is our author's assertion that from the name Thulis that of the mysterious northern island, the Ultima Thule was derived! Mr. Graves may be a theologian and philosopher, but he is not "up" in philology.

"Alcestos," whom he would have us believe to have been a female saviour, laid down, or offered to lay down her life for her husband, when told by an oracle that he could never be cured of a disease unless one of his friends died in his stead. Some accounts represent her as rescued at the last instant by Hercules. Alcestis or Alceste, as she is sometimes called, is the heroine of a drama by Euripides, and of a modern opera.

Atys, of Phrygia, was a shepherd beloved by the goddess Cybele. She made him a priest, imposing on him a vow of celibacy. This he violated, and being made delirious by the incensed divinity, castrated himself.

Crite, of Chaldea, is affirmed by an imaginative writer from whom our author has derived the main thread of his work, to be set forth in the sacred books of the Chaldeans, as a crucified god, a redeemer and atoning offering, etc. It is enough to say that we have found no mention of him in the investigations of such modern archæologists as George Smith, nor in the admirable summary of Babylonian beliefs and history in the latest edition of the Encyclopædia Britannica.

Wittoba, an incarnation of Vishnu, is the same as Chrishna. Bali is another of the divinities with which, under various names *later* Brahmanism has swarmed. Iao, of Nepaul, who Mr. Graves thinks may have been the original of the Hebrew Jehovah! is probably one of the Jins or deities of the Jains, a heretical sect of Northern India, who have mingled Buddhism and Brahmanism with strange conceits of their own. Indra, of Thibet, is a Buddhistic transformation of Indra, the sky god of early Brahmanism, and later the personal opponent of Chrishna. Mr. Graves has cited at second or third hand the reports of uncritical mediæval Christian missionaries concerning these latter deities.

Prometheus, a thoroughly mythical character, who was nailed to a rock on Mt. Caucasus—not on a cross—where a vulture was perpetually to feed on his ever growing liver, was rescued by Hercules, after thirty years of torment. He is an interesting character, but it is hardly fair to quote a dramatic poet of the fifth century before Christ, as authority concerning a person who, if he had ever lived at all, must have flourished at least a thousand years earlier. We have thus reduced the catalogue to Mithra and Chrishna, or Krishna, as the best authorities spell the name. With them we shall deal later, as they, especially the last named, are the chief dependence of Mr. Graves, and the school of writers of which he is the exponent.

MR. GRAVES' SCHOLARSHIP.

The reader has already been furnished with some interesting glimpses of Mr. Graves' scholastic attainments, and it is only just to him, as well as the public, that their full extent should be known.

He himself tells us in the introduction to the "Saviors" that "ignorance of science and ignorance of history are the two great bulwarks of religious error." It is well, therefore, to be certain that our guide is thoroughly conversant with the paths through which he proposes to lead us, in urging us to desert the well trodden road of old fashioned beliefs. It certainly does not inspire confidence to find so few of his "saviors" answering the description he gave at the start, and we are puzzled, to say the least, by further information which he vouchsafes us.

What must one think, who has looked over the plates of unintelligible hieroglyphics in Lord Kingsborough's Mexican Antiquities, to find one set referred to as if it were a printed volume—as an "ancient work called Codex Vaticanus," in which "the immaculate conception is spoken of as part of the history of Quexalcote, the Mexican Savior"? Is it possible that Mr. Graves has never seen the Codex, or the great work in which it is reproduced?

Again, he regards Alcides and Hercules as two different persons, when they are the same. In another place he refers to Alcides as an Egyptian, and Prometheus as a Roman god! Are all the classical writers and lexicographers wrong, or has Mr. Graves been corrected by "spiritual" influences?

He represents Confucius as miraculously born, when, in truth, he was the son of his father's second marriage, and was the soberest of matter-of-fact men, a kind of Chinese Ben Franklin, who discouraged religious enthusiasm, taught practical morality on purely earthly considerations, and died very unromantically at a good old age. The great Jew Maimonides is styled Mamoides, and Ludwig Feuerbach, whose name the author ought to know, since he professes to quote him, is called Mr. Fleurbach. It is very careless, if not very dishonest, to claim that Herod had fourteen thousand babes massacred at Bethlehem, or more strictly to assert that that number perished, if Matthew has written the truth. There were not anything like fourteen thousand men, women and children, all told, in Bethlehem and its "coasts." The village was a little one, and a dozen children under two years old would be a fair estimate.

But his errors are not confined to surmises. He thus garbles Gibbon: "In a note to chapter XV, he (Gibbon) says, 'It is probable that the Therapeuts (Essenes) changed their name to Christians, as some writers affirm, and adopted some new articles of faith." Gibbon really says: "Basnage * * * * has examined with the most critical accuracy the curious treatise of Philo, which describes the Therapeutæ. By proving that it was composed as early as the time of Augustus, Basnage has demonstrated, in spite of Eusebius (b 11. c 17) and a crowd of modern Catholics, that the Therapeutæ were neither Christians nor Monks. It still remains probable that they changed their name, preserved their manners, adopted some new articles of faith, and gradually became the fathers of the Egyptian ascetics."

On page 62, Iao, of Nepaul, appears as Jao Wapaul, a god of

THE GOSPELS NOT BRAHMANIC. 21

Britain. The next example of our author's intelligence is very rich. He says: "We will first hear from Colonel Wiseman, for ten years a Christian missionary in India." Then follows a quotation from Cardinal Wiseman's lectures on Science and Religion!

I was surprised that Mr. Graves should misrepresent Gibbon, for if there is honor among thieves there surely ought to be fair dealing between skeptics. Having discovered this rule disregarded, I was prepared to find him slandering an apostle. We are coolly told that Paul, in Romans iii. 7, justifies falsehood when he says: "If the truth of God hath more abounded through my lie unto his glory, why yet am I also judged as a sinner?" Why does not Mr. Graves quote the next verse, " And not rather (as we be slanderously reported, and as some affirm that we say) 'Let us do evil, that good may come', whose damnation is just." Are misquotation and perversion among the methods of breaking down the "bulwarks of religious error?"

Occasionally his malice gets the better of his consistency. On page 304 ("Saviors") he quotes some verses in eulogy of forgiveness from the "old Persian bible," which say:

> "Forgive thy foes nor that alone;
> Their evil deeds with good repay:
> Fill those with joy who leave thee none,
> And kiss the hand upraised to slay."

To this he adds:

"The Christian Bible would be searched in vain to find a moral sentiment or precept superior to this. Certainly it is the loftiest sentiment of kindness toward enemies that ever issued from human lips, or was ever penned by mortal man. And yet is found in an old heathen bible. Think of 'kissing the hand upraised to slay.' Never was love, and kindness, and forbearance toward enemies more sublimely expressed than in the old Persian ballad."

On page 347, he talks differently. After citing the text: "Love your enemies," he adds:

"Then what kind of feeling should we cultivate toward friends? And how much did he love his enemies when he called them fools, liars, hypocrites, generation of vipers, &c? And yet he is held up as 'our' example in love, meekness and forbearance. *But no man ever did love an enemy; it is a moral impossibility, as much so as to love bitter or nauseating food.*"

The italics are my own. The charming harmony of sentiment should be duly credited to Mr. Graves.

Referring to resurrections, we are informed that personages declared by the author to be Egyptian gods, "Tyndarus and Hypolitus, were instances of this kind, both (according to Julius) having been raised from the dead." Who was Julius? Hippolytus, not Hypolitus, and Tyndarus were both personages in Grecian mythology; the latter being the father of Helen. Mr. Graves may have had access to better authority, perhaps.

We have also the very novel information, on the alleged evidence of "Col. Hall and Dr. Oliphant," that "no drunkenness, no fighting, no quarrelling, no thefts, no robberies, no rapes, no fornication, no domestic feuds or broils, and no fraudulent dealing take place in Japan." I should prefer to examine these authorities for myself rather than take Mr. Graves' word for it. If they say any thing of the kind, they contradict other writers, and what the mails so frequently bring in the way of accounts of rebellions, assassinations and wide-spread immorality. So much for the "Sixteen Crucified Saviors," and the author's learning. We have by no means exhausted the fountain, for there remains an abundant supply in both volumes, to some of which we shall apply analytic tests in other connections. We have made it very evident, however, that Mr. Graves is neither well informed nor honest. We shall next proceed to examine the trustworthiness of the authorities on which he has principally relied.

HIS AUTHORITIES.

A casual glance at both books, especially the "Saviors," will show, that, with much trash and many repetitions, they contain a good deal of curious learning, "important if true." Where did the author get it? The blunders we know are his own, but all is not stupidity. He has been candid enough to say regarding the "Saviors," and the remark is in part applicable to the "Bibles," "Many of the most important facts, were derived from Sir Godfrey Higgins' Anacalypsis, a work as valuable as it is rare." He would not have exaggerated had he admitted that the bulk of his data was borrowed from this source. Had he been more exact, however, he would not have given Mr. Higgins the prefix "Sir." He was an English country gentleman of studious habits, born in 1771, and dying in 1833, before his Anacalypsis, in two volumes quarto, saw the light. He was previously well known to antiquaries by his "Celtic Druids," a work of much research but eccentric conclusions. The Anacalypsis is a vast muddle of undigested information, gathered from all sources, good, bad and indifferent, and shaped to suit his preconceived theory. It is regarded by scholars as curious, but as absurd in argument. Mr. Higgins, though learned, was incapable of weighing authorities. The sub-title of the Anacalypsis is "an Attempt to unveil the Mysteries of the Saitic Isis." Now, it happens that the Saitic Isis was not veiled. Plutarch thus quotes the inscription on the temple of Neith [probably the Egyptian prototype of Athene or Minerva] at Sais: "I am that was, and is, and is to be; and my veil no mortal hath yet drawn aside." Whether Neith or Isis was the embodiment of the divine wisdom which Mr. Higgins endeavored to solve, it is certain that even skeptical scholarship recognizes his utter failure. He was childishly credulous, "believing everything but the Bible."

His theory is that of Dupuis, with modifications. Dupuis a French astromoner, born 1742, died 1809, reached the opinion that all the religions of antiquity rose from nature-worship, and that their mythologies were allegories of celestial phenomena. The sun, the twelve signs of the zodiac, and the precession of the equinoxes solved every problem. He included Christianity, holding that the alleged birth of Christ, on the 25th of December, was only the passage of the sun from the winter to the vernal solstice; that His mother was the constellation Virgo; Simon Peter, Aquarius, and so on. Other nations had typified the same processes under different names from time immemorial. Everything began, however, in Egypt. This wild idea is not wholly destitute of fact as applied to some of the ancient heathen systems. Its fault is that it inverts the pyramid. The nations worshiped the sun, moon, and stars, first as the dwelling places of divinity, and afterwards as deities; but their mythologies were largely distortions and exaggerations of real, earthly events which were subsequently ascribed to the heavenly bodies, first typically but finally in good faith, at least, among the masses. Absurd as the system of Dupuis must seem, it had a temporary success. Volney popularized it in his "Ruins," and others adopted it in part or as a whole, but it is now obsolete, except among ignorant infidels of the Boston Investigator and Graves stamp.*

Applied to Christianity it involves the assumption that the early Christian Martyrs died for their belief in a Master whom they very well knew never existed.

Mr. Higgins was a great admirer of Dupuis. He borrowed much from him, and declared that the priests hated his "Origine de Tous les Cultes," so much that it was very scarce and hard to get.

---

* This remark is perhaps too sweeping, though it would have been true a few years ago. After slumbering for more than a generation since the death of Sir William Drummond, Mr. Higgins and others of their class, men with some pretensions to learning, though with small claims to common sense or fairness, like Goldziher and Inman, show a disposition to retrace some of the abandoned paths. They are agreed only in their desire to prove the scriptures unhistorical, for they differ much in both theories and details. The sun myth hobby is partly responsible for this revival of old speculations.

That was forty-seven years ago. I procured without difficulty in Paris last summer, a copy of the unabridged work in three volumes, quarto, with an atlas of plates for just $5. There were plenty more to be found, and the abundance and cheapness show the esteem in in which the book is now held. The greatest blow that Dupuis ever received was the discovery that the zodiacs of Esneh and Denderah, which according to his astronomical plan ought to be many thousand years old, only date back to the Roman emperors, and are younger than our era.

This was a fact which Mr. Higgins disliked to acknowledge, but he was wary, and so selected India as the mother of all mythologies. Abraham himself, he says, was a fugitive from Brahma land. He had suffered in a war between the worshipers of the female principle and those who reverenced the male. He retained much of the old system which adored the sun under various incarnations or avatars. When Mr. Higgins wrote, Buddhism was believed to be older than Brahmanism, a theory that is now as obsolete as his philology. According to the Surya Siddhanta, a famous Indian mathematical treatise, which Mr. Higgins held to be of very remote antiquity, and which the Brahmans claim to be inspired, and a million years old, the equinoctial point moves eastward one degree in six hundred years, and as often as this change occurred it was thought that an incarnation took place. Among these, Krishna the eighth avatar of Vishnu, was the most famous in India, while others of the "Saviors" had the same reputation in the various countries to which Brahmanism had been carried. Thus, actually, living persons might be falsely endowed with divine honors at each cycle. Sakia, the real historic Buddha, was according to Mr. Higgins, the ninth Indian avatar, following Krishna at an interval of 600 years. To Jesus Christ, a Jewish reformer, the same ascriptions were made by Jews who had been proselyted to beliefs borrowed by the Essenes from the east. A consideration of this process will show how the author of the Anacalypsis, and Mr. Graves, after him, explain the alleged frequent appearance of " crucified saviors" throughout the ancient world. According to them, Indian mythology had penetrated almost everywhere, and people were sun-worshipers often without knowing it. Everything that was supernatural in all religions came from the scheme of cycles. We know very well that supernatural legends were abundant in the old world, and that heroes were often endowed with supernatural attributes by the credulous multitude, but they were not generally Saviours in the usual sense of the word, much less crucified ones, as we have already seen.

KRISHNA.

Of all the avatars, or incarnations, Krishna, whose name Mr. Graves spells Chrishna, Mr. Higgins, Cristna, and another skeptic, Christna, was the most important. Indeed he is the one whom the infidels of a past generation endeavored to set up as the prototype of Christ. They attempted, as we have seen, to increase the similarity of the names, but the resemblance is more apparent than real. Christ, as we hardly need say, means the anointed. Krishna signifies black. When, however, the English first became acquainted with oriental literature, ninety or one hundred years ago, they discovered coincidences which were very startling. Believing as some of them did, that the story of Krishna dated back hundreds of years before the Christian era, there were points that were exceedingly troublesome. Krishna was the eighth, and first complete avatar of Vishnu; those which preceded him being mere emanations. One object of his incarnation was "the destruction of Kansa, an oppressive monarch, and, in fact, an incarnate Daitya, or Titan, the natural enemy of the gods." Kansa was the cousin of Devaki, the divine, Krishna's mother, who was married to a nobleman named Vasadeva. Vasadeva had another wife named Rohini. Devaki had had six children, and hearing that she was about to have another, Kansa seized her and her husband and put them in prison. Vishnu, however, interfered, and transferred the unborn child, who was Balarama, Krishna's future playfellow, to the womb of Rohini, who was still at liberty. Devaki's eighth child was Krishna, so he could hardly be said to be born of a virgin. Celestial phenomena, including a great light and the visit of an angel choir, accompanied the birth. Kansa pursued the child, but its father escaped with it, and, on reaching a river, the infant commanded it to open a passage, which it did, a serpent meanwhile holding its head over the youthful divinity as a kind of umbrella. His father exchanged him for the child of a cowherd, returning to the palace with the latter. Kansa, Herod-like, gave orders for slaying all the male children in the neighborhood. Krishna meantime grew up among the peasants, joining in all their sports, marrying several of the girls, and being very licentious in appearance, if not in reality. Like Apollo, he was master of the lyre, and serpents and beasts were beguiled by his melodies. He overcame the great serpent, Keliga, and trampled on its head. In later years he is said to have cleansed lepers, raised the dead, descended into the invisible world, and reascended to the proper paradise of Vishnu. He finally conquered Kansa, fought in a battle which lasted eighteen days, twirled a mountain on his little finger, stole a famous tree from heaven, and performed other incredible deeds. Rukmini was his favorite wife, but he had sixteen thousand others, each of whom bore him ten sons. He had been warned to beware of the sole of his foot. As he sat one day in the forest, a huntsman, Jura (old age), mistook him for a beast and mortally wounded him in his foot. Another legend has it that he was nailed to a tree by the arrow, and that he foretold before dying, the miseries which would take place in the Kali Yuga, a wicked age of the world, thirty-six years after his death. So great a light is said to have proceeded from his dying body that heaven and earth were illuminated.

It would be absurd to say that the life of Krishna parallels that of Christ, but still there are some striking similarities. What is the explanation? If we are to believe Higgins and Graves, the Krishna story, as I have epitomized it above, dates back to 1200 B. C. The latter asserts in his "Bibles:"

> "In times coeval with the earliest authentic records, says a writer, the Hindoos calculated eclipses, and were venerated for their attainments in some of the arts and sciences! According to the learned astronomer Baily (he means Bailly) their calculations in astronomy extended back to the remote period of seventeen hundred years before Moses, and some of the ancient monuments and inscriptions of India bespeak for its religion a very remote antiquity. Some of our modern learned antiquarians have expressed the opinion that the Sanscrit language of the Brahmans is the oldest language that can be traced in the history of the human race. They also state that this language was extant before the Jews were known as a nation; and neither it nor their religion has *ever* been known to *change*. These facts are sufficient to establish the existence of the Brahman and Buddhist systems of religion long prior to the earliest records of the Jewish nation."

A greater amount of absurdity and falsehood could hardly have been compressed within so few lines. Yet much of what is said was believed by Mr. Higgins, and forms the basis of his hypothesis. We mention as a well known fact that Hindoo religion found its earliest expression in the Vedas, so called from Ved, the law. There are four of these, the oldest being the Rig Veda. They are believed to have come immediately from God. Each consists of two parts, the first called Sanhita, comprising hymns, prayers and ceremonies for sacrifice and oblations; the second called Brahmana, in which the first cause, creation of the world, moral duties, precepts, punishments, etc., are set forth. They have a number of supplements and commentaries. Many of the hymns are sublime, but there is a decided leaning toward pantheism. There is some doubt as to their age. Bunsen, always extravagant on the side of antiquity, thought that some of the hymns might have been composed three thousand years before Christ. Prof. Whitney of Yale College, the leading Sanscrit scholar in our country, inclines to 2000 to 1500 B. C.; Max Mueller, the translator of the Rig Veda, thinks the hymns were collected in their present form from twelve hundred to one thousand years before Christ, though composed earlier. It must be noticed that the Vedas have nothing to say of a trinity composed of Brahma. Vishnu and Siva, or of any incarnations. Brahma was then neuter, scarcely personified. In the Institutes of Manu. a later compilation, there is the first trace of the modern system of gods.

Next comes the grand period of the great epics, the Mahabharata and the Ramayana. pre-Christian, but with many comparatively modern interpolations and changes. An episode of the former recounts a dialogue between Krishna and Arjuna, whom he is serving as charioteer. This episode is known as the Bhavagat-gita. The Krishna legend has now become established. It does not contain, however, the most striking points of resemblance to the gospel naratives which we have summarized, and yet the Bhavagat-gita is held to be post-Christian by leading scholars, some assigning it to the first, and others to the third century of our era. It is in the Puranas, and in one of the most recent of them, the Vishnu-Purana, regarded by some as only three or four hundred years old, by others relegated to the twelfth century, that it appears full blown. Granting the utmost that can be demanded, the features, on which Mr. Graves lays chief stress are post-Christian; probably stealings from the apocryphal gospels, which we have good reasons to believe were circulated in India in the early Christian centuries. There was much trade between that country and the west, and Nestorian missionaries visited it before the Puranas attained their present form.

INDIAN ANTIQUITY AND LITERATURE.

As to the age of Hindoo literature I shall first quote the late Ebenezer Burgess's able "Antiquity and Unity of the Human Race." He was a clergyman and missionary to be sure, but Mr. Graves frequently cites the Rev. D. O. Allen, another missionary, so he cannot object to the class. Besides, Mr. Burgess was a member of the American Oriental Society, author of a Marratta Grammar, and co-translator of the Surya Siddhanta, an Indian mathematical work already mentioned and to which reference is made in the "Saviors." He says:

"The earliest Hindoo writings and the earliest astronomical observations on record cannot be *proved* to have had an earlier date than the fourteenth or fifteenth century before Christ, though a few hundred more may be conceded as probable. The oldest astronomical treatise, which has been regarded as an important witness against the Bible, is proved incontrovertibly to have been composed some four or five centuries after Christ. And as the work of bringing to light the ancient literature of the Brahmans proceeds, the tendency among European scholars is to bring it within more and more modern limits.

This tendency to modernize is sometimes, doubtless, allowed to proceed too far. But, however, this may be, this fact may be regarded as established, viz: that the ancient literature of India affords no materials for disproving the truthfulness of the Bible; on the contrary, it contains much that corroborates the claims of the sacred volume to a divine authenticity."

I will furnish him with a still more radical citation from that most eminent secular authority, Klaproth. He says in his Memoires Relatifs a l' Asie:

"The astronomical tables of the Hindoos, to which a prodigious antiquity has been attributed were constructed in the seventh century of the common era, and were posteriorly reported by calculations to an anterior epoch."

We thus see what becomes of the Surya Siddhanta and its revalations regarding the cycles. Furthermore, the antiquity which Messrs Higgins and Graves claim, is based on the speculations of Bailly, a French astronomer of the last century, whom even Voltaire believed to be wild. Laplace, an unbeliever, and the greatest astronomer of his day, was equally convinced of the absurdities of Bailly's scheme. He says:

"The origin of astronomy in Persia and India is lost, as among all other nations, in the darkness of their ancient history. The Indian tables suppose a very advanced state of astronomy; but there is every reason to believe that they can claim no very high antiquity. Herein I differ with pain from an illustrious and unfortunate friend." [Bailly was guillotined in the first French revolution.]

Other eminent astronomers coincide with Laplace, and it is a common if not dominant belief that the Indians derived their astronomy from abroad.* More than this, a noted

* See Postscript.

English astronomer, Mr. Bentley, taking the statements of the Janampatra or horoscope of Krishna, which contains the position of the planets at the time of his birth, found that the heavens could only have been as there described on the 7th of August A. D. 600. This shows that the astronomical calculations respecting him are comparatively modern. What then is left of Mr. Higgins' cycles?

But we are told that Alexander the Great heard the name of Krishna when in India in the fourth century before the Christian era. This is granted, though Arrian who tells the story, lived in the second century of our era. We do not ignore the fact that there may have been an ancient hero, about whom legends gradually clustered. Yet the Puranas, which are almost the sole authority for the life of Krishna, so far as it resembles that of Christ, are known to be modern. The Bhavagat-gita, as we have said, is referred to the first and third centuries after Christ, while the Puranas which furnish the most startling and numerous coincidences, are as says, H. H. Wilson in his "Religion of the Hindoos," not " anterior to the eighth or ninth centuries and the most recent not above three or four centuries old." That relating especially to Krishna, which supplies most of our account of him, has been conceded by Brahmans as the production of Vopadesa, who flourished in the twelfth century of our era. If any resemblances between Christ and Krishna seem to exist in the older versions, after due excision of the later accounts has been made, we may give the parallelism all the weight it deserves and suffer nothing. As Hardwick says in his "Christ and Other Masters:"

"If Krishna was violently persecuted in his infancy, it might be answered, so was Hercules exposed to the implacable rage of Juno. If Krishna, in his triumphs comes before us crowned with flowers, the description will apply to Bacchus also. If Krishna, veiling his divinity, is said to have been concealed beneath the roof of Nanda, the cow-herd, Apollo, in like manner, acted like an ordinary mortal, when he sought a shelter in the household of Admetus. Or if, again, Krishna is to be regarded as a purely human and historical hero, doomed to death in childhood from forebodings that his life would prove the ruin of another, we can find his parallel in the elder Cyrus, who had also been intrusted to the care of herdsmen to preserve him from the vengeance of his royal grandfather, whose death it was foretold he should eventually accomplish."

We have said enough about Krishna, we should think, to satisfy a reasonable person that if any parallelism exists between him and Christ, it was not borrowed from the Indian hero. It should also be noticed that it is only by a stretch of the imagination that Krishna can be said to have been crucified. Further, there is no doctrinal likeness. As Hardwick well says:

"The most perfect incarnation of Vishnu, as found in Krishna, is docetic merely; it rather seems to be than is. According to the theory of matter which prevailed among his followers, the divine and human could not truly come together, and could not permanently co-exist. The one essentially excludes the other. Krishna, therefore, on going back to his celestial home, or in the language of philosophy, on his re-absorption into the Great Spirit of the universe, entirely lays aside the perishable flesh which he had once inhabited. * * * In this respect, he differs altogether from the God-man of the Christian Church, the Mediator in whom divine and human are completely reconciled."

Mr. Graves has asserted that the Hindoo religion has never changed. We have already indicated the absurdity of this statement. There has been, even leaving out of account the great Buddhist schism, as every tyro in oriental literature knows, a complete and constant departure from nature-worship to a pantheon crowded with millions of divinities, and from a simple ceremonial to the grossest and most barbarous rites. It is the same process which has taken place in all lands where God in His unity has been abandoned. The first chapter of Romans describes the downward road in perfectly vivid language.

We read, in the article on Brahmanism, in the latest edition of the Encyclopædia Britannica:

> "Buddhism appears to have been the State religion in most parts of India during the early centuries of our era. To what extent it became the actual creed of the body of the people it will probably be impossible ever to ascertain. One of the chief effects it produced on the worship of the old gods was the rapid decline of the authority of the orthodox Brahmanical dogma, and a considerable development of sectarianism. Among the great variety of the deities of the pantheon, Siva, Vishnu, and Parvati have since claimed, by far, the largest share of adoration, and it is in special accounts of the Saira, Vishnaro, and Sakete sects, rather than in an exposition of the Brahmanical belief, that the religious history of India, from about the beginning of our era, can be dealt with satisfactorily. At that time, the worship of Vishnu in his most popular avatar, in the person of Krishna, appears to have received much countenance at the hands of the priests, with a view of counteracting the growing influence of Buddhism. The sectarian spirit gave gradually rise to a special class of works, the modern Puranas composed for the express purpose of promoting the worship of some particular deity. In the seventh century, the authority of Sakyamouni's (Buddha's doctrine was already on the wane. * * * Siva does not occur in the Vedic hymns as the name of a god, but only as an adjective in the sense of kind auspices. Vishnu occupies a place in the Vedic mythology, though by no means such a

place as would entitle him to that degree of exaltation implied in his character as one of the three hypostases of the divinity. * * * As the language of the Aryan Hindoos has undergone continued processes of modification and dialectic division so their religious belief has passed through various stages of development, boldly distinguished by certain prominent features."

The Suttee is comparatively modern. The Rig Veda tells the widow to go home from her husband's funeral rite and resume her duties.

This is sufficient to show that Mr. Graves' Sanscrit studies must have been undertaken under very unfavorable circumstances. We should expect such mistakes from a man who alleges Horace Greeley as authority for the statement that there is "no doctrine of Christianity but what has been anticipated by the Vedas!"

ANOTHER OF MR. GRAVES' AUTHORITIES.

I have said that "Higgins' Anacalypsis" is Mr. Graves' chief authority in regard to the "Saviors," and other points; but he is not the only one. We have frequent unacknowledged flings from "Paine's Age of Reason," for which Bishop Watson's "Apology" is a sufficient antidote; and more from that very dishonest and ill-tempered work, Taylor's Diegesis, a treatise which makes Krishna the prototype of Christ, and accepts as true the blunder of Eusebius in reckoning the Essenes as the original Christians—an idea repudiated by the great mass of the Christian Church, ancient and modern, as by the able skeptic, Gibbon, already quoted. Taylor recanted his infidelity in later life, and so may be regarded as having abandoned his untenable hypothesis. No modern writer of eminence has confounded the Essenes with the Christians, save DeQuincey, the eccentric opium eater, and Taylor's assertions regarding Krishna have been overthrown in our criticisms of Higgins and Graves.

There is another writer, however, from whom the latter appears to have borrowed largely in his "Saviors," and to whom he does not give due credit. That writer is M. Louis Jacolliot, whose "Bible in India" has helped Mr. Graves to fill his pages of alleged coincidences between the lives and teachings of Krishna and Christ, and between the names of Old Testament and Vedic characters. Regarding the former, he is frank enough to say in a note what most men would dislike to confess:

"The author deems it proper to state here with respect to the comparison between Christ and Chrishna, that some of the doctrines which he has selected as constituting a part of religion of the Hindoo Savior, are not found in the teachings of that deified moralist. But as they appear to breathe forth the same spirit, it is presumed he would have endorsed them had they come under his notice."

I have not room to examine all Mr. Graves' pretended exposition of Krishnaism and its parallelism with Christianity. Instead of doing so, I shall simply bring evidence as to the utter worthlessness of the authority on which he has based his statements. Mr. John Fiske, whom he should accept as an impartial judge since he is is one of the most zealous advocates of the "science" which is to overthrow the Bible, says in a review of Mr. Gladstone's "Juventus Mundi:"

"But the whole subject of comparative mythology seems to be terra incognita to Mr. Gladstone. * * The only work which seems really to have attracted his attention is M. Jacolliot's very discreditable performance called 'The Bible in India.' Mr. Gladstone does not, indeed, unreservedly approve of this book; but neither does he appear to suspect that it is a disgraceful piece of charlatanry, written by a man ignorant of the very rudiments of the subject which he proposes to handle."

But I have a still more important witness against M. Jacolliot, and as his testimony is very curious and interesting, I shall be excused for reproducing it at considerable length. Max Mueller, the eminent philologist, whose authority on oriental literature is second to none, has published a paper on "A Chapter of Accidents in Comparative Theology." After recounting many of the mistakes into which learned men have fallen in their attempts to discover similarities between the Biblical narratives and the various heathen mythologies, and showing the fallacy of identifying totally different personages, historical or fabulous, from some resemblance between their names, and instancing the errors of Sir Wm. Jones, he continues:

"It was under these influences that Lieut. Wilford, a contemporary of of Sir William Jones, as co-laborer took up the thread which Sir William Jones had dropped. Convinced that the Brahmans possessed in their ancient literature the originals not only of Greek and Roman mythology, but likewise of the Old Testament history, he tried every possible means to overcome their reserve and reticence. * * * The coyness of Pandits yielded. The incessant demand created a supply, and for several years essay after essay appeared in the Asiatic Researches, with extracts from Sanscrit MSS, containing not only the names of Deukalion, Prometheus, and other heroes and deities of Greece, but likewise the names of Adam and Eve, of Abraham and Sarah, and all the rest. * * At last, however, the coincidences became too great. The MSS. were again carefully examined, and then it was found that a clever forgery had been committed, that leaves had been inserted in ancient MSS., and that on these leaves, the Pandits, urged by Lieut. Wilford to disclose their ancient mysteries and traditions, had rendered in correct Sanscrit verses all that they had heard about Adam and Abraham from their inquisitive master. Lieut. (then Col.) Wilford did not hestitate to confess that he had been imposed upon." Mr. Mueller continues : " As long, however, as researches of this kind are carried on for their own sake, and from a mere desire of discovering truth, without any ulterior objects, they deserve no blame, though for a time they may lead to erroneous results. But when coincidences between different religions are searched out simply in support of preconceived theories, whether by the friends or enemies of true religion, the sense of truth, the very life of all science is sacrificed, and serious mischief will follow without fail. Here we have a right, not only to protest but to blame. There is on this account a great difference between the books we have hitherto examined and a work lately published in Paris by M. Jacolliot, under the sensational title of *La Bible dans l'Inde; vie de Jesus Christna*. If this book had been written with the pure enthusiasm of Lieut. Wilford it might have been passed by as mere anachronism. But when one sees how its author shuts his eyes against all evidence that could tell against him, and brings together without any critical scruples whatever seems to support his theory that Christianity is a mere copy of the ancient religion of India, mere silence would not be a sufficient answer. Besides, the book has lately been translated into English, and will be read, no doubt, by many people who cannot test the evidence on which it purports to be founded."

Mr. Mueller tells how M. Jacolliot, who was a judge at Chandernagore, from studying the ancient holy books of the Hindoos, became convinced that our civilization, our religion, our legends, and our gods, have come to us from India, after passing in succession through Egypt, Persia, Judea, Greece and Italy. He found the Old and New Testaments in the Vedas, and quotes texts which allege that Brahma created Adima (in Sanscrit the first man), and gave him for a companion Heva (in Sanscrit, that which completes life.) Our author continues:

"But much more extraordinary things are quoted by Jacolliot from the Vedas and the commentaries. In one passage of the Vedas we are told that the ancient poet exclaimed, 'Woman is the soul of humanity.' On page 63 we read that Manu, Minos and Manes had the same name as Moses, &c. * * * It has been remarked with some surprise that Vedic scholars in Europe had failed to discover those important passages in the Veda which he has pointed out, or still worse, that they had never brought them to the attention of the public. * * * It is simply the story of Lieut. Wilford over again, only far less excusable now than a hundred years ago, and decidedly reprehensible on account of the author's unscientific bias. Many of the words which M. Jacolliot quotes as Sanscrit, are not Sanscrit at all; others never have the meaning which he assigns to them; and as to the passages from the Vedas (including an old friend, the Bhaga veda gita), they are not from any old Sanscrit writer—they simply belong to the second half of the nineteenth century. What happened to Lieut. Wilford has happened again to M. Jacolliot. He tells us the secret himself. 'One day,' he says, 'when we were reading the translation of Manu by Sir W. Jones, a note led us to consult the Indian commentator Kutiska Batha, when we found an allusion to the sacrifice of a son by his father prevented by God himself, after He had commanded it. We then had only one determination to find again in the dark mass of the religious books of the Hindoos, the original account of that event. We should never have succeeded but for the complaisance of a Brahman, with whom we were reading Sanscrit, and who, yielding to our request, brought us from the library of his pagoda the works of the theologian Romet Savias, which yielded us precious assistance in this volume.' As to the story of the son offered as a sacrifice by his father and released at the command of the gods, continues Mr. Mueller, M. Jacolliot ought to have found the original account of it from the Veda, with text and translation, in any history of ancient Sanscrit literature. He would soon have seen that the story of Sunschepa being sold by his father in order to be sacrificed in the place of an Indian prince has very little in common with the intended sacrifice of Isaac by Abraham. M. Jacolliot has, no doubt, found out by this time that he has been imposed upon, and, if so, he ought to follow the example of Col. Wilford, and publicly state what has happened. Even then, I doubt not that his statements will continue to be quoted for a long time, and that Adima and Heva, thus brought to light again, will make their appearance in many a book and many a lecture room."

This expectation has been abundantly realized in Mr. Graves' volumes. Will he acknowledge his error now that it has been made known to him on unimpeachable authority?

BUDDHISM—THE ZEND-AVESTA.

The reader has perhaps had enough of Mr. Graves. The utter worthlessness of his authorities relative to Brahmanism has been demonstrated, and his glaring incompetency to separate truth from falsehood has been made equally apparent. Yet his assertions on some other departments of his subject must not be passed over. We can afford to be brief with his attempt to confound Buddhism with Christianity. Their doctrines are entirely different; the one making nirvana or annihilation by absorption into divinity the end of all, and denying any personality to the Supreme; while in the other "life and immortality are brought to light." There are legends that Buddha was born of the Virgin Maia, but they can be traced no nearer than several hundred years after his death, and several centuries after Christianity was established. The Buddhist romancers simply adopted Christian facts into their own mythology. There is no resemblance between the ascetic life and natural decease of Buddha, and Christ's miraculous career and violent death. We know that Mr. Higgins has attempted to prove that both Krishna and Buddha were crucified, but he has to pass off Roman Catholic pictures taken by the Portuguese to India as heathen productions, and quote unsupported legends to make even a fair show for his case.*

The Zend-Avesta or Zenda-Avesta, as Mr. Graves improperly calls it, means Avesta — text, and Zend translation, commentary, or paraphrase. It is the ancient Parsee Bible proper; but the Sadder, which our author calls its New Testament, is only a summary of Parsee doctrine.

He says also, "The historical facts to establish the Persian religion long prior to that of the Jews are numerous, cogent and unanswerable. They have calculations in astronomy, which scientists admit must have been made four hundred years anterior to the time of Moses. According to Berosus, fragments of their history have been found which extend it back fifteen thousand years; and he tells us it is computed with great care." This, as far as the scientists are concerned, is decidedly novel, and if the statement of Berosus is to be believed, they disagree with him, since there is a vast difference between fifteen thousand years and four hundred before Moses, which last would carry us back to about the time of Abraham. Berosus was a priest of Belus at Babylon, and historical

* See Postscript.

writer who lived in the fourth century before Christ. He is not a very ancient authority, and not a very trustworthy one. He claimed for his own Chaldea an antiquity of 2,150,000 years, so that his statements respecting Medo-Persia are at least to be taken with allowance. Many have thought that Zoroaster was a contemporary of Darius, but it is generally believed that he lived much earlier. He is supposed to be the author of some parts of the Zend-Avesta, but not of all, and much of the original work is lost. Hardwick ("Christ and Other Masters") says:

"One chief result of modern exploration in this region of philology has been to demonstrate that whether as preserved in the original, or as translated by Parsees, the treatises of the Avesta *in their present* shape can date no farther back than the Sassanian revival in the time of Artaxerxes, or the third century of the Christian era, (A. D. 226.) Another of these results has tended to confirm and justify suspicions with regard to the antiquity of several writings which are commonly adduced as high authorities by modern Parsees. Of one important work (the Bundehesh) we may affirm with certainty that it had never existed in the Zend or elder dialect of Persia. * * * * *

Such criticisms are not, of course, intended to deny that many chapters of the Persian sacred works have been actually committed to writing as early as 400 B. C., for 'books of Zoroastrians' are related to have perished at the time of Alexander's expedition. Many, also, of the sacred chants and ceremonial precepts, many as now existing, have originated at the epoch of the first migrations. Yet, while granting this, our ablest scholars seem to be persuaded more and more that works which have been brought together in the Avesta, are not only the productions of different ages, but have all been modified and modernized by the intrusion of fresh matter."

To the same effect we might quote other authorities, but Hardwick is inferior to none in his field. It is true that in the Zend-Avesta the narratives of the temptations, the fall of angels, etc., have a closer resemblance to the Biblical statements on the same subject than most other ancient records. Yet they are mingled with much that is degrading, and the collection lacks the historical form of the Hebrew Scriptures. The unity and personality of God, the grand peculiarity of our Bible, is wanting. We have instead the dualism which makes Ormuzd the good, and Ahriman the evil deity. We cannot be sure that the resemblances to the Bible were not derived from intercourse between the Jews and their Persian masters in the captivity, or even in post-Christian times; since, as we have seen, the Zend-Avesta in its present form is no older than the third century of our era. Again, assuming the truth of Genesis, we should be prepared to expect certain coincidences of traditions. A deliverer is promised there, and though the nations that "forget God" were suffered to go on in the path of wickedness which they had chosen, with minds constantly becoming more blind through the influence of the hardening of the heart which sin always brings, they could not wholly forget primeval revelation. History is full, not of "Crucified Saviors," but of man's consciousness of sin, and desperate longings to make peace with the "great first cause least understood," but of whom the visible universe so plainly testified that they were without excuse for their misdeeds. Plutarch says that many cities are without walls; some without temples, but none without an altar. Whence came this universal belief in the necessity of sacrifices and blood atonement? Was it the product of man's imagination and fears, or was it, even in its gross perversion, such as the immolation of human beings, a survival of the faith by which Abel offered up the firstlings of his flock? The conscience of men to-day, of the learned and refined, as well as of the ignorant and coarse, utters the same teachings. Yet Mr. Graves says the "Bibles" were all written when man was animal rather than intellectual, and that he has now out-grown such conceptions. On the contrary he himself is a living witness to the truth of what we have stated. He cannot rest. He is constantly berating Christianity and asserting that it is dead, but the spectre will not down. His boastings are like the whistlings of the superstitious man as he passes through a grave yard after dark, the proof of his apprehensions.

All Christians recognize in the heathen dogmas the workings of man's sense of sin and the vague traditions of the fall and the promised helper. They know, however, that the latter first appeared in the One who said, "I am the way, the truth and the life"—not as did Plato, Socrates and others, that He was the disciple of truth. We well know that sublime ethical doctrines are scattered through the writings of the ancient sages. They are mixed, however, with much that is false; were held largely as theory and not as rules for practice, and exerted comparatively little influence on the lives of the masses. The Chinese quote more often than they observe the version of the golden rule enunciated by Confucius; the morals of Seneca, the brother of the Gallio who "cared for none of these things," are not unlike those of his contemporary the apostle Paul, yet the former was the toady of Nero, and his writings are known only to scholars. The latter counted all lost for Christ, and is remembered and copied, not for his ethics, but for the divine sanction by which they were established. There is much moral wisdom in heathen teachings, but more inconsistency and folly. The gospel, *i. e.* the good *news* from heaven, is found only in our Scriptures. Mr. Graves may sneer at all this. He cannot affirm however that the Jews learned of the Persians, for much of the Old Testament is as old if not older than the hymns of the Zend-Avesta, and all of it dates back centuries before the existing form of the Persian work. Moreover its teachings have a living and irrefutable illustration in the history and condition of the Jewish people.

MITHRA.

The later forms of religious thought in Persia developed a kind of mediator in the person of Mithra. He was the highest of the twenty-eight second class divinities of the ancient Persian pantheon. He was god of the day, and. in a higher sense, of light, presiding over the movements of the principal heavenly bodies. The meaning of his name is a friend. He was the protector of man in this life and in the next. Omniscient and all-hearing, he ran his course unceasingly between earth and heaven, and with his club beat off Ahriman, or the great principle of evil and his subordinates, the daevas.

His mysteries were attended by fearful initiatory ordeals and human sacrifices were perhaps connected with his worship in some cases. Mithraism was finally suppressed in the Roman empire, A. D. 378. Mithra was represented as a beautiful youth with a Phrygian cap, kneeling upon a bull, into whose neck he plunges a dagger. Allegorical emblems of the sun surround the group, the bull being at the same time attacked by dogs, a serpent and a crab. The mysteries were celebrated at the spring equinox, March 25th, and Mithra's birthday was December 25th, the day fixed when the Church had become formal and borrowed observances from heathenism which it transformed to its own uses, as the natal day of Christ. This change involved no acceptance of the original rites. All evidence points to early April as the true date of the Saviour's birth. There is no doubt that Mithraism exerted some influence on Christianity, after the latter had lost its primitive simplicity, but it is absurd to believe, as Dupuis endeavors to prove, that our religion is a branch of Mithraism.

In this pretence Mr. Higgins, and of course Mr. Graves, concur. The most they can claim is that some early Christian apologists exaggerated certain points of resemblance between their own faith and Mithraism, in order, we may suppose, to help on the conversion of adherents of the latter cult. The Manichean heretics endeavored to blend Mithraism with Christianity. For a time their influence was extended, but they soon passed into obscurity. The same change of dogmas is obvious in Parseeism as in Hindooism. In early days Mithra was wholly subordinate to Ormuzd. The Zend-Avesta describes him as his creature and tributary. In the early Christian centuries he was declared to have been generated by the sun either from the rock or soil—not from a virgin, as Mr. Graves affirms, and there is no pretense of his having been crucified.

SOME LAST WORDS.

Mr. Graves also describes the Chinese sacred books which are mere treatises on practical morality; the Koran, largely borrowed from the Scriptures and which apparently confounds Miriam, the sister of Moses, with the Virgin Mary; the book of Mormon and several minor works deemed inspired by some, but says nothing of them which demands attention, and I therefore pass them over, to give a little space to the more personal characteristics of his "criticism." It is very singular, however, that he does not include in his list the Chaldean "Genesis" which gives an account of the Creation, the fall and deluge much like that of Moses, yet obviously an independent and somewhat "heathenized" version of the same great sacred tradition handed down in our Scriptures.

I have reviewed the theories which he has borrowed from abler men than himself, and shown that they are not new, and that they fail to prove that there ever were "Sixteen Crucified Saviors" even in popular belief. His attempted establishment of coincidences in their doctrines as well as their births and deaths, being founded on the same evidence as the latter, falls also to the ground. Of his own additions and assumptions it is difficult to say whether they most expose his impudence or his ignorance. It is very evident that he is not competent to form a candid judgment. His treatment of the Old and New Testaments shows a degree of passion, a wilful blindness, and an unfairness that defeats itself. Granting for the sake of argument that the inspiration of the Scriptures is a doubtful matter, they are venerable for age and contain much that is beautiful in thought and expression. Yet our author can see nothing of this, but detects contradictions and absurdities everywhere. He has prepared a long list of discrepancies for the "Bibles,," and promises more of the same sort. In their compilation he has evidently been indebted to a pamphlet filled with passages strained and garbled for a similar purpose, that was published in Boston some years ago. Did he ever see the Rev. J. W. Haley's masterly exposure of that brochure, called an " Examination of Alleged Contradictions," etc.? If he has not, I advise him to procure it, before going further. A consultation of the Bible itself will be enough to show that many of his so-called contradictions do not exist. There are obscure and seemingly discordant passages in the Scriptures, but most are susceptible of explanation and adjustment, and none are of great importance. He has decidedly overshot his mark. If the Bible be indeed such a nonsenical and immoral book as he contends, it is strange that none but men of loose doctrines, if not of loose lives, have discovered the fact? Will Mr. Graves himself be hurt by a close observance of the ten commandments? Is it immoral to enjoin purity of thought as well as act? We have never seen a more signal exemplification of the "evil heart of unbelief" than in the man who charges the Scriptures with indecency yet frequently indulges in profane and indecent jests. And this master of all science refers in his "Bibles" to Isis, the chief female deity of Egypt, as "him!"

Mr. Graves believes either that Christ never existed, or that all that was supernatural concerning Him is falsehood. He ought now to be convinced that Krishnaism affords him no ground for unbelief. He must go elsewhere than India for support in his skepticism. Will he tell us how the unparalleled character of the Son of Man was invented? He may not agree with Rousseau who pronounced it God-like. What has he to say of this tribute by a fellow unbeliever, of rare talent, John Stuart Mill?

"And whatever else may be taken away from us by rational criticism, Christ is still left, an unique figure, not more unlike all his precursors than all his followers, even those who had the direct benefit of his teachings. Who among his disciples, or among the proselytes, was capable of inventing the sayings ascribed to Jesus, or of imagining the life and character revealed in the gospel? Certainly not the fishermen of Gallilee; as certainly not St. Paul, whose character and idiosyncracies were of a totally different sort; still less the early Christian writers, in whom nothing is more evident than that the good which was in them was all derived, as they all profess that it was derived from the higher source."

Mr. Graves does not believe in prophecy. He asserts that Tyre was not taken by Nebuchadnezzer as predicted. That is a point disputed among scholars. Has he ever read Volney's description of the modern village on its site, in which that unbeliever unconsciously, we suppose, used about the exact words of scripture in saying he saw only a few rocks covered with fishermen's nets. He tries to explain away the destruction of Babylon by the fact that a small settlement exists near by. He does not grapple, however, with the fifty-third chapter of Isaiah and its announcement that the man of sorrows should "make his grave with the wicked and with the rich in his death:" unintelligible until centuries later, when Christ, after being crucified between two thieves, was laid in the sepulchre of Joseph of Arimathea. He is silent regarding the predicted dispersion of the Jews. He omits to notice the prediction that Bethlehem should be the birthplace of the Messiah. I might greatly extend this list, but I have said enough on this point.

He limits the proof of Christ's existence pretty much to the statement of Tacitus that Christ was crucified under Pontius Pilate. This is sufficient in itself, and pronounced unimpeachable by Gibbon, though assailed by the dishonest Taylor. But this is not all. Martial, Suetonius and Pliny bear witness to early Christianity or its founder. The text of Josephus, which Mr. Graves sets aside as wholly spurious, is held by Gieseler and other German historians to be only partially interpolated; and then Josephus certainly writes of John the Baptist, and confirms various statements in Acts. The Roman catacombs afford a vast mass of evidence in favor of the authenticity of the early Christian records. Mr. Graves himself in one place admits on Lardner's testimony that the gospels were written a few years after the death of Christ, while elsewhere he repeats the silly story that the New Testament books were first voted inspired at the Council of Nice, about A. D. 325. Is he ignorant of the fact that Irenæus, A. D. 185, declared that there were four gospels; that he and his contemporary, Tertullian, quote or refer to the gospels about four hundred times, and that two-thirds of the New Testament is found cited in the works of Origen, A. D. 185 to 254? Theophilus, A. D. 169, composed a commentary on the four gospels. The gospel of Matthew was circulated in India between 175 and 190. The Muratorian Canon, about 170, which is mutilated at the beginning, after an apparent reference to Mark, mentions Luke as the third, and John as the fourth book. The epistle of the Churches of Lyons and Vienne 177, quotes from Luke, and from the gospel and first epistle of John. In the writings of Justin Martyr, Hermas and Barnabas, running back to the beginning of the second century, there are frequent New Testament passages. In those of Clement, of Rome, born about the time of the crucifixion, are many expressions corresponding with the utterances of the first three gospels. The voting of which our author makes so much, was the due attestation of the writings which had always been recognized as canonical, in order that the apocryphal imitations might be assigned their proper place.

Paul in the fifteenth chapter of first Corinthians, an epistle which the most skeptical German writers have been compelled to admit as genuine, declares that there still survived many of five hundred Christians who had seen Christ after his resurrection. The story might be incredible, but it was believed; credited in the face of persecution, infamy and death. Would men have rushed by hundreds and thousands to certain destruction if they had not had reason for their faith?

Mr. Graves does not believe in miracles, unless in the wretched tricks of his spiritualistic confreres, yet all the early adversaries of Christianity, heathen as well as Jewish, admitted that Christ worked them. They ascribed them to magic and other absurd causes, but the Talmud, Celsus, Porphyry and Julian were all in accord on this point. Mr. Graves may prefer the revelations of mediums and rappers, but the majority of those who have been born to the privileges of Christendom and many who listen to the teachings of the missionaries which Christendom sends forth, will find consolation in life and support in death from the old, old story. A recent traveler in heathen lands says he found no new temples—the superstitions that built them are going to decay, and the edifices will, sooner or later, follow them. Christianity, on the other hand, in spite of the dissensions, the follies, the coldness and the unfaithfulness of its followers, is still living, still spreading, and will grow brighter and purer until there comes to it the light of the perfect day.

J. T. P.

Cincinnati, Jan. 25th, 1879.

MR. GRAVES' REPLY.

A REVIEWER REVIEWED.

To the Editor of the Telegram:

When I learned that an extensive review of my works was to appear in the *Telegram*, I conjectured that it would be from the pen of some bigoted sectarian, whose creed had been cast in some theological institution, and that it would consist of a string of dogmatic assertions, without much evidence, or the citation of historical authorities. But I confess myself happily disappointed. It is for the most part one of the most fair, candid, and apparently truth-seeking criticisms I have ever seen from the pen of a Christian writer. And I feel certain that if we do not agree in our conclusions as the result of our investigations, we can agree on friendly terms to disagree. It is true, he indulges in one or two cases in rather unfriendly language, and makes rather unfriendly charges. But if he has any grounds for this, he will not have when he reads my defense and explanation. He seems to call in question my "scholastic attainments," my respect for the truth, and my moral reputation, or moral character. As for my scholastic attainments, I beg leave to say that I never claimed to attain to any eminence in scholarship, having never spent a day in my life in a college as a student. I graduated in a log hut about ten feet high, roofed with poles and clapboards. With respect to my character for truthfulness, I will only say that there are men in the city of Richmond and vicinity who have known me for more than fifty years, and if any of them have ever suspicioned me of being guilty of a willful departure from the truth, I have never learned the fact. As for my character in other respects, as shown by my practical life, I will assume the liberty to say that I am willing to have it compared with that of my reviewer, or any clergyman in the United States, and promise to show as clear a record. An investigation of my practical life will show that I have lead an honest and industrious life, and have been strictly temperate in my habits. I never, knowingly, wronged a man out of a dollar; never had a fight, nor even serious quarrel, with any person; never indulged in profane swearing; never got drunk, nor swallowed a dram of any kind of intoxicating liquors, nor swallowed enough of intoxicating beverages of any kind, or of all kinds put together, to make a dram. And lastly, I never took but one chew of tobacco in my life, and that I repented of in less than a half an hour, and I promised my God if I lived through it I would never take another. And that promise I have never broken. If my reviewer can present or exhibit a better practical life than this, he will command my highest esteem as a true, moral man, and I have no reason to doubt but that he is such a man, if he does not award me the same honor. As for reputation, in the popular sense, I never aspired for popular favor. I never courted either popularity or notoriety; and if I had, my personal appearance would have been a bar in the way of attaining it. I have led such an obscure life, and am so unprepossessing in my personal appearance, that perhaps, as the editor suggests, I am better known at home than abroad. These things have not escaped my observation. Perhaps; I might say with Tom:

> "Says Dick to Tom your character is bad,
> I've heard it from many.
> You lie, said Tom,
> I never had any."

Perhaps, I have not much character or reputation of any kind. My main object has been to lead an honest, useful, and truthful life, whatever evidence my reviewer may suppose he has found to the contrary. And I admit, he does cite one case which does seemingly sustain his charge of misrepresentations in quoting history—one case of alteration in the four thousand citations which I have made—the case of Gibbon. But this matter I will explain satisfactorily when I come to it. With this much preface and personal defense allow me to say I am glad the review has been written and published, because it presents the popular church view of the question, which has been presented substantially to the public a hundred times before, by different writers, and thus furnishes the readers of the *Telegram* an opportunity of seeing and examining, (when collated with my version of the matter) both sides of the question. And I am perfectly willing to rest the case with the verdict of the reading public, knowing that truth will triumph sooner or later. And here allow me to suggest, that it is a matter of importance that we should know what we are trying to discuss, and clearly understand the ground of difference between us. Otherwise, we may in our ignorance of each other's views and positions, waste much time and paper in arguing points we are both agreed on. And, this I observe, my honest and gentlemanly reviewer has inadvertently done.

A large portion of his article is occupied in arguing points that I have never doubted or disputed. And consequently, my reply will not occupy the space in the *Telegram* which his article does, while at the same time I shall notice every point of any importance, on which we differ. I cannot escape the conviction that he has not read my books very thoroughly, as he charges me, in some cases, with omitting what I have inserted with great care, and in other cases of believing or disbelieving, what I have not only denied, but attempted to disprove. For example, he says: "Mr. Graves does not believe in prophecy." Here is a most signal blunder. I have repeatedly, in both my large works avowed my belief in prophecy, and cited many examples of prophecy and their literal fulfillment "to the very letter," in both works. For proof, see page 298, of "The Sixteen Saviors," and 122d of "The Bible of Bibles." Here, then, is one point settled.

Again, after representing me as being an enemy of the Bible and "berating Christianity," he says: "The Bible contains much that is beautiful in thought and expression. Yet Mr. Graves can see nothing of this." Here is another serious mistake. On page 28 of "The Bible of Bibles," he will find the following language:

"There are in all Bibles beautiful veins of thought coursing through their pages, and they contain many moral precepts, which are in their nature, elevating and ennobling, and, which if practically lived up to, would do much toward improving the morals of the people and enhancing their happiness." And on page 64 it is stated with respect to the Christian Bible, that, "There is scarcely a book, or even a chapter in the whole Bible, that does not evince a spirit of religious devotion, and an effort for the right, and the prophets often breathed forth a spirit of the most elevated poetry." And elsewhere, it is stated that the Bible is a very useful book in its place, and that I have no objection to urge against the Bible, but only to the improper use to which it is applied, etc.

Now, this certainly does not evince a spirit of hatred for the Bible, as my reviewer represents. Having incidentally noticed these points, I will now try to follow my reviewer in regular order. He faults me for my scholarship, because I spell some words differently from some of the authors which he has read, and also for using wrong words. But here he commits several rather laughable blunders himself in his efforts to correct me. Cobb, says: "Before a person assumes the office of teacher or critic, he should be certain he has studied the subject far enough to dispel his own ignorance."

He attempts to correct me for using the word "exposition" and says I mean "exposure." But here he is mistaken, I mean exactly what I say. Webster, Walker and Worcester all define "exposition" to mean "the act of exposing," and that was exactly what I was attempting to do. His criticisms with respect to spelling foreign and Oriental names leads me to conclude that his reading of history has not been as extensive as I at first supposed. His reading seems to have been confined to a few favorite, authors, and some of them, not very reliable. Otherwise he would know, and should know, that there is no uniform standard for spelling scarcely any foreign names. Take for example, the God of the Hindoos, whom he calls Krishna, and assumes this is correct. And yet some of the missionaries and Oriental scholars, who have lived in that country and studied their language, spell the word Kreshna, or Kreeshna, and others Krishnoo, and others again Chrishna and so on. There are not less than seven ways of spelling this word. And authors differ in their mode of spelling other foreign names in the same way. He says that Quexalcote should be Quetzalcoatl. But I prefer the English, while he gives the Aztec mode of spelling the word. It appears he is ignorant of the fact that the word has been translated. Again he says, the Celtic God whom I call Eros, "is not Eros but Esus." But I prefer to take that standard authority, the New American Cyclopedia, for authority in the case, which declares it was Eros, unless he can show, he has got ahead of that work, written by and endorsed by all the learned men of the age

Fleurbach is a typograhical error. I have the work and have seen the name a hundred times, and know how it should be spelled. He certainly commits a serious blunder in leaving out a syllable when he uses the word Bahavatgita. I have consulted eleven authors, and they all spell it Baghavatgita, as I have in my books. And I might cite other examples to show that his philological wisdom is hardly competent to criticise and correct scholarship. And I might say of him as he says of me, "he is not much of a philologist."

But I must hasten to more important points. He wades through an almost interminable sea of Oriental legends and traditions to show that my crucified gods all died a natural death, except those, perhaps, who were mere fabulous beings. But all this is a work of supererogation, so far as I am concerned. I admit the whole of this detail substantially. It contains no new ideas and no new facts. The same or a similar history of those gods, can be found in almost any common work on heathen mythology. I have nine authors who relate substantially the same history of those gods my reviewer has written out. Our libraries are well supplied with works of this character, which relate pretty much the same story of these Oriental gods. I not only admit this, but I also admit they may be as reliable as the history of them, which I have presented in "The World's Sixteen Crucified Saviors." That is for the authors to settle, and not for me. The secret of the whole matter is; two very popular and learned authors, who have investigated and studied the subject more critically than any other writers, who ever wrote on the subject, claim to be able to throw new light on the subject. They claim, just as Max Muller does, with respect to the Hindoo vedas, to have discovered that changes and alterations or omissions were made many years ago in the histories of the Oriental gods, by which some of the most important events of their lives were either left out or materially altered. Those two authors are Alexander Dow and Sir Godfrey Higgins. (All the English writers I have seen prefix Sir to his name, my critic to the contrary notwithstanding).

Higgins, who devoted twenty years to the investigation of the subject, presents an imposing array of facts to prove that an important chapter in the history of many of the Oriental gods, being written by interested representatives of other religions, was left out, either accidentally, or from interested motives. He cites one very striking case in proof and illustration, which is made a matter of record, by the authority of the British parliament. A deputation which was sent out by the British to examine the laws, polity, and political and religious institutions of India and other Oriental countries, learning in India, the curious story of their incarnate god, Chrishna, they made notes of it in their report. But as these notes were thrown together hastily without any arrangement, on leaving the country, they placed them in the hands of a learned Roman Catholic bishop, at Calcutta, with instructions to arrange them together in chronological order, and send them to London. But it was found, when they came to be examined, after they had reached that city, that they had been materially altered — whole chapters were missing, and the most important events of his life, such as his immaculate conception, his crucifixion, resurrection, ascension, etc., were entirely left out. It was so seriously mutilated that the committee would not endorse it. And Mr. Higgins says that the Roman Catholics have perpetrated similar frauds with respect to other religions. And these frauds being committed before the histories of some gods, now in circulation, were written, we consequently have not the full history of their fabulous lives, as most, if not all of them must be supposed to be.

My critic could have saved all the labor in attempting to show those gods were not crucified by simply reading the note appended to the chapter on crucifixions in "The World's Sixteen Crucified Saviors," page 119, where I have stated: "There is much ground to doubt whether any of those crucifixions ever took place, or were ever realized as actual occurrences. It must be borne in mind that a great deal of ancient history is mere fable. Many things related as actual occurrences were designed for mere symbols. Many of the ancient Christians argued that this was true of even Jesus Christ — that some of the principal events recorded in his life were never realized as actual occurrences, and were not intended to be so understood, but were designed to be understood in some spiritual sense."

The moral lesson designed to be taught by the chapter on crucifixions (as stated in my note, page 119,) is simply that the belief or idea of the crucifixion of gods was prevalent in various Oriental countries long before the reported crucifixion of Christ, and whether fact or fiction, is a matter of no importance, if we could determine. It would not affect my position in the least, if it could be shown that the gods were all fabulous beings, (as many of them probably were,) and that the story of their crucifixions were sheer fabrications. It was not the fact, but the mere conception of the crucifixion of gods, that I aimed to establish. Some of them, which were stated as mere fiction, came to be looked upon by many as a matter of fact. It may be asked if I accept these stories of crucifixion as fiction, why I have related them as a matter of fact, and assigned a date for their occurrence? That question is easily answered. My note shows that it was the belief of their disciples, and not my own, I was giving. I have assumed no more license than writers on romance always do — that of relating imaginary events as real. I have nowhere stated that I accept or endorse the cases of crucifixions as facts. I have stated on page 118, that I believe they were invented, and for what purpose they were invented. They are designed to teach an important moral lesson.

My learned critic ridicules the idea of Ixion having been crucified as an actual occurrence. And so do I. And yet it is apparently related as a matter of fact, with a spiritual significance. In some cases, other beings were crucified with the gods — one being arranged on each side, as in the case of Christ. This also has a symbolical or spiritual signification.

Take for example, the Celtic story of a god being crucified with a lamb on one side and an elephant on the other. The elephant was designed to represent the magnitude of the sins of the world, being the largest animal then and there known, while the lamb was designed to represent the innocency of the victim—*i. e.*, the god offered up. Here we have "the lamb of God taking away the sins of the world." Here is another spiritual lesson. And whether the god was crucified or not, does not in the least affect the moral of the story.

Of course I do not believe any more than he does that a lamb or an elephant, or that Apis (which I learned when a boy, is the Latin term for bull), was ever crucified, even though millions in past ages may have believed it.

My learned and gentlemanly critic says, "Chrishna was not crucified, but died a natural death at the age of about eighty." That may be, but why does he say so? Because he has found the statement in some author which he has read! But will he be as reasonable with respect to Christ, whom some, even Christian authors, and a number of the early Christian churches and thousands of the most pious and devout primitive Christians, stoutly maintained was never crucified! Even that author whom he quotes himself as being a reliable and unimpeachable authority, (Ireneus), denies he was ever crucified. This learned and pious bishop declared upon the authority of the martyr, Polycarp, who claimed to have got it from St. John and the elders of Asia, that Christ was not crucified, but lived to the age of about fifty. Here, then, are two accounts of Christ, as well as of Chrishna. If he accepts the story of the crucifixion of one, why not the other? or if he rejects that of Chrishna, why not that of Christ, also—seeing we have contradictory stories in both cases. This brings me to notice the very senseless expedient which he drags in to prove that the story of Chrishna is a mere transcript of that of Christ.

Of all the ridiculous and silly subterfuges ever invented to save a sinking cause, and proving the truth of the proverb, "that drowning men will catch at straws," that of dragging the ancient Hindoo god, Chrishna, down into the sixth century of the Christian era, is one of the most laughable, if not tragical, ever put on record. I hope my respectable critic will not accept this as personal. It is not intended for him. He did not invent the story. It was invented long before he was born, by an arrogant, self-conceited, pedantic student of divinity, by the name of Richard Bently, whom my critic calls an astronomer (God save the mark!) I have never seen a work on astronomy that so much as mentions his name. He resorted to the silly farce of attempting to show by the senseless rules of astrology, that the planets point to the six hundredth year of the Christian era as the time of Chrishna's birth, an assumption so foolish and senseless that his own friends laughed at him, and finally laughed him out of it, and he gave it up. It is so thin that I was astonished when I found that my learned critic is disposed to endorse it, and it almost compelled me to doubt his good sense, or else his honesty. The evidence is so voluminous to prove that Chrishna figured in history long before the birth of Christ, that any person who should express a doubt of it in the presence of any Oriental scholar, outside of the Christian ranks, would be laughed at.

Another very weak expedient which my critic drags in as evidence, that the life of Chrishna was borrowed from that of Christ, is the foolish story that Max Muller has found a few forged leaves in one of the vedas. (Muller he spells Mueller, but the New Cyclopedia, the best authority in the world, spells it Muller. Here he is beat again). I call this story foolish, because even if true, it can amount to nothing.

When Horace Greeley asserted that all the doctrines of Christianity can be found in the Hindoo vedas, (which the Rev. D. O. Allen, twenty-five years a Christian missionary in India, admits to be at least 1000 years older than Christianity) he did not mean it could all be found in one volume of the vedas. They are scattered through the five volumes. And my 456 striking analogies in the life and doctrines of Christ and Chrishna are not the half of them taken from the vedas, but from the other Hindoo books, and from the various volumes of the New American Cyclopedia, much better authority than Max Muller, professor in the old English orthodox university of Oxford.

Sir William Jones, whom the New American Encyclopedia pronounces the greatest linguist and Oriental scholar ever known, and who was at the same time a devout Christian, and who lived and died in India, obtained a more critical and profound knowledge of the Hindoo religion than any other scholar who ever wrote on the subject. We will hear what he says on the subject. He says, " that the name of Chrishna and the whole outline of his history were long anterior to the time of our Savior, and probably to the time of Homer, we know very certainly." (Asiat. Res. Volume 1st, page 254). Now mark, he says. "we know very certainly"—no guess about it. To suppose that he was deceived in the matter by a few false pages of history stuck in one of the vedas would be the climax of nonsense, for the vedas proper, don't say a word about this god. It is found in other sacred books, and not only in the books, but engraved and inscribed on old time-worn rocks, much older than the books, and whom all the Oriental scholars who ever examined them, I believe, pronounce much older than Christianity.

When that English writer, Mr. Moore, wrote his work called "The Hindoo Pantheon," in which he inserted a great many drawings, representing the crucifixion of the god Chrishna, with the cross and the print of the nails in his hands and feet, made by nailing him to the cross, also the mark of the spear in his side—all drawn from sculptured drawings, found on some of the oldest-looking rocks and rock temples in India, none of the Christian professors, who labored so hard with him to keep him from publishing these facts, ever denied but that they were much older than Christianity, or they would not have opposed it. They were not drawn from the vedas or any other books, but from solid porphyry rock, bearing evidence of being several thousand years old. That great orthodox historian, Mr. Goodrich, puts the quietus on this matter, and settles the question forever, by telling us that the first Christians and Christian missionaries who entered India and China, were very much astonished to find a religion so strikingly similar to their own in both of those countries, and could only account for it by supposing that the devil anticipating the coming of Christ, got out a system of religion just like his. That is, he got out the second edition of the gospel plan of salvation before the first edition had been published, which certainly proves him to be a very smart chap, thus to outwit God Almighty.

Now, as this occurred long before the alleged alterations in the Hindoo sacred books, it settles the matter forever as to their being forged, and especially in the case of China, where no alterations are claimed to have been made. And hundreds of other similar facts might be cited if I had room for them, to prove the superlative nonsense of trying to make out that the Hindoos borrowed their religion from the Christian gospels. It is too thin. Even that bigoted misssionary, D. O. Allen, who lived among them twenty-five years, don't claim it.

I come now to notice an alleged contradiction in one of my books, with respect to loving enemies. First statement:—

"Forgive thy foes, nor that alone,
 Their evil deeds with good repay;
Fill those with joy who leave thee none,
 And kiss the hand upraised to slay."

Second statement: "No man ever did love an enemy. It is a moral impossibility, as much so as to love bitter or nauseating food." It seems strange, passing strange, that any person can see any contradiction in these two statements. The first statement says not a word about loving enemies. It speaks of forgiving them, filling them with joy, repaying their evil deeds with kindness or kind treatment, the very acts I have recommended in both of my books, and the very acts I have recommended as a substitute for loving enemies in the very next sentence after the statement that it is impossible to love them; which my critic should have been fair enough to have quoted. "Treat thine enemy kindly and thus make him a friend," is my advice, which is the sentiment I have so highly commended in the Persian moral system. "When I say "they gave utterance to the loftiest sentiment that ever issued from human lips," I make no allusion to their loving enemies, for they say nothing about it. And let it be understood, it was not the feeling that prompted Christ to enjoin love to enemies that I criticised, but the philosophy. The feeling may be a noble one, and yet unphilosophical and impracticable of execution. I did not mean to show that Christ was not a philanthropist, but that he was no philosopher to enjoin what is impracticable. To settle the matter in a few words, I will put two questions to my critic: 1st. Can you treat enemies with respect, repay their evil deeds with kindness, the sentiment of the first statement? You will say yes. 2d. Could you love an enemy while beating you unmercifully and smashing your face into a jelly out of sheer spite, or while abusing your wife before your eyes? If you say *no*, then the question is settled. If you say yes, I will prove by Webster that you are mistaken. Webster defines love as a verb, to mean "to be pleased with," and love as a noun, to mean "an affection of the mind toward an object which excites pleasure or pleasurable emotions." Could the cruel and brutal treatment of yourself or wife excite pleasurable emotions in your mind? You are compelled to say no, and that settles the question again. Then where is the contradiction, when you yourself admit both statements to be true? Let it not be understood that because we can't love an enemy, we should therefore hate him; nothing of the kind. We may, by treating them kindly, excite their love toward us so that we may finally come to love them.

I will now notice the case of the alleged misquotation of Gibbon. It appears as my friendly critic has presented it, that I have made Gibbon say exactly the opposite of what he did say, or intended to say. I will only say that if I did commit such an error it must have been corrected, for I do not find it as he has quoted it, in the last edition of the work. And I will also say that I shall feel profoundly thankful to my critic for any errors he can find and report in either of the books. And I will never let another book be bound up till the error is corrected. While the book referred to was going through the press, I was traveling in Minnesota, so that I had no opportunity to correct typographical errors, or errors made by the lady who copied it for the press. And when it came out, I found a great many errors had been made in my historical quotations, by leaving out or putting in words so far as I had the works from which I had quoted in my possession. But many of the historical works I used had been hired or borrowed and returned to the owners, so that I could not examine the correctness of the quotations made from them till I could obtain them, which, in some cases was very difficult, and in other cases impracticable.

Higgins' large work, from which I have quoted very largely, and which I hired from a gentleman in New York, at an expense of five dollars, I have not been able to get hold of since I returned it. Nor have I seen Gibbon's work since my book was first published, and from which I made several quotations. But I will obtain it and see if any errors have been made by the copyist or type-setter. I have corrected more or less errors in every edition of the work that has been issued, as fast as I have succeeded in getting hold of the numerous works from which I have quoted that are not in my library. And if I have overlooked an error made in quoting Gibbon relative to the Essenes, it was because on reading it I supposed it to be his real sentiments, and I suppose and believe so yet, notwithstanding he appears to deny it in this case. But other quotations made from him show very plainly that he did believe the Essenes were the original Christians, notwithstanding he appears sometimes to deny it. So that if the copyist or type-setter, by leaving out a sentence or part of a sentence, did misrepresent his language they evidently have not misrepresented his real sentiments; so that not much harm is done after all.

I intend to show hereafter by quotations from his writings what his real sentiments were in the case, when I get hold of them again. I have made it a rule, in both of my works, to shorten quotations from history when I could do so without perverting the meaning. But I did not, in any case, designedly misrepresent an author. Indeed, it would have been foolish for me to have done so, knowing that I would soon be detected, especially if perpetrated on a work as well known as Gibbon's, which is in nearly every library, both public and private.

A man would be the greatest fool imaginable to attempt to perpetrate a fraud on a work as common and as well known as Gibbon's, with the idea that he would not be found out in less than a month, or at least a year; and then as there are, in this case, many better witnesses to prove the same thing, it would be unnecessary to force him into a lie to prove it. It can easily be seen that there was less motive for misrepresentation in this case than in most of the other five thousand historical citations found in the three books. This explanation must satisfy every candid and unbiased reader, that no misrepresentation or perverted quotation was intended. And if any is found, no time will be lost in correcting it. No person could be more mortified than I was to find more than a hundred typographical errors in the first work, and about thirty in the last work, ("The Bible of Bibles"). They cannot be found in the last edition of it, however.

Referring to a number of these typographical errors such as Mamoides for Maimonides, Colonel for Cardinal, and several other cases the critic says, "We know these blunders are his own." Now this is rather a broad and bold assumption of knowledge on his part, and withal it seems to me rather uncourteous and does not sound very well in a writer who has committed the several blunders with respect to names and words I have pointed out in this article, and who, after condemning me for using the word "exposition," uses it himself in the same sense. But I can excuse him by supposing that the work of criticising is something new to him. I will only say further on this point that I think I have committed no errors in either of my works. The typographical errors referred to above were marked by me for correction but somehow overlooked by the publishers.

To avoid trespassing upon the columns of the *Telegram*, or the liberality of its kind and indulgent editor, I will notice the other objections with which my reviewer attempts to demolish me, in the briefest and most succinct manner possible. In speaking of my estimate of the number of children destroyed under Herod (14,000), my reviewer says, "It is very careless, if not very dishonest in Mr. Graves to claim that Herod had 14,000 babes slain. There was not anything like 14,000 men, women and children all told in Bethlehem and its coasts. A dozen children under four years would be a fair estimate." Here is a wonderful stretch of historical knowledge which demolishes all the standard historical works on eastern Asia I ever read, and throws all commentators overboard. The New American Cyclopedia, the standard authority for the world, says that

Herod the Great was, for some time governor of Gallilee, and afterwards at the instance of Mark Antony, the Roman senate made him king of all Judea. His decree extended to "Bethlehem and all the coasts around about." This is very indefinite, but it must have comprised an extent of many miles, and a population of many thousands. At least, this is the view more than one-half of Christendom have always had of it. And it is to their learned men I am indebted for the estimate of 14,000. So that the reviewer must settle the matter with them. This estimate of 14,000 was made by learned orthodox Christians, and not by me. The most learned men of the most orthodox church in the world (the Greek church) made this estimate only a few hundred years after the massacre is said to have taken place. (See Haywood.) And I guess more than one-half of Christendom have believed it ever since. Hence it will be seen that there have been many millions of "very careless and very dishonest" men and Christians besides Mr. Graves, and sound, orthodox Christians at that. I have never known any Christian writer to put the number less than 8,000. Now I will not retort upon my reviewer, and say he is either "very careless, or very dishonest" to put the number at a dozen, but will use the softer word ignorant. I have noticed this objection at greater length than I should have done, because I am accused of being dishonest in putting the number at 14,000 instead of the glaring and self-evidently absurd number of twelve. The idea is laughable.

2. The reviewer tries to make sport of my assigning Salavahana to Bermuda. He seems to suppose that I have reference to a cluster of West India Islands, called the "Bermudas" when I don't even use the name. It is Bermuda, not the "Bermudas." I speak of a small province as appears in ancient Burmah.

3. He asks, when I quoted Paul about lying for the glory of God, why I did not quote the next verse about not doing evil that good may come of it. I answer because it is on a different subject and has no direct connection with the first verse. It commences: "And not rather," etc., which shows it is not the same thing, and not intended to teach the same doctrine.

4. He says my boastings about the new discoveries in theology are like the whistlings of the superstitious man while passing through a grave yard. Here he is mistaken. My whistling was done while a good orthodox church member, when I read Horace Greeley's statement that all the doctrines of Christianity can be found in the old heathen Hindoo bible (the Vedas). It alarmed and shook my orthodoxy so badly, that I had to whistle to keep up courage; and also when I found that phrenology traces man's evil actions to the brain instead of the devil.

5. He says: "All evidence points to early April as the true date of the Savior's birth. If all the evidence points to that date, then the twenty-fifth of December has been celebrated for hundreds of years as the real time, without any evidence of its being such; and would not that prove they were either very ignorant, or "very

careless, or very dishonest." This paragon of wisdom should have been born a few hundred years sooner, so as to stop the vast waste of time and money in celebrating the twenty-fifth of December.

6. He says, Prometheus is a mere fabulous character, on whose liver vultures are represented as feeding for thirty years, while nailed to a rock. I know that is the story told in our popular works on heathen mythology, which I read when a boy. But Mr. Higgins says, "I have seen the account which declares he was nailed to a cross with hammer and nails." Ana., Vol. 1, page 327. He pronounces the first story a dishonest fabrication.

7. My reviewer says, " Mr. Graves charges the scriptures with indecency, yet constantly indulges in profane and indecent jests." Here is another egregious mistake. I never indulged in profane language in my life; never uttered a profane oath, or used a profane word. Nor did I ever indulge in indecent or vulgar language. It is so repulsive to my nature that I studiously avoided, when writing my books, quoting the vulgar language of the Bible, even when referring to the many texts which contain such language. Doubtless the Bible writers meant nothing wrong in the case, and such language was not repulsive to them, but it is to me.

8. He admits there are discordant and contradictory passages in the Bible, but says they were not important. Dear me, what a stretch of credulity. I have cited 277 contradictions, and have shown that there is scarcely one doctrine, principle, or precept in

the Bible, or an important event that is not referred to by contradictory statements, thus rendering it absolutely impossible to learn anything with certainty about them. And yet I will not say these contradictions were always in the Bible. I am objecting to the Bible as it is and not as it may have been. It was under the control of the Roman Catholics for nearly a thousand years. And I have cited more than a dozen Christian writers in "The Sixteen Saviors," who declare the Bible has been thoroughly changed since it was first written. So that even if it were right once, it can't be right now.

9. He tells us that Robert Taylor repented of his infidelity before he died. Well, that is news. But it can't be true, whoever may have started the report. He died in an apoplectic fit, so that he had no time to repent. And, besides, he was about the last man in the world to repent of anything. With firmness and self-esteem almost unbounded, he feared nothing, and was as stubborn as a mule. It would take something more than thunder and lightning to change such a man's views.

10. Criticising my language when I speak of religious nations, he asks, "Were there ever any irreligious nations?" Such a question discloses a greater ignorance of history than a man who assumes the high prerogative of a critic should possess. There have been many irreligious nations. Livingstone, in his African explorations, names several nations or tribes who manifested no knowledge or belief in religion of any kind; such as the natives of the Arru Island.

11. He speaks of the ascension of Christ being witnessed by 5,000 disciples. I would ask how that could be, when, according to the Acts, 1, 15, written after that time, the number of disciples was only 120. What had become of them? Had they relapsed back into heathenism?

12. He faults me for considering the few lines referring to Christ in Josephus an interpolation and a forgery. But this is not an infidel assumption. The most eminent modern Christian writers are with me in this position. That able Christian author, Dr. Lardner, who has written ten volumes in defense of the Christian faith, and which may be found in nearly all Christian libraries, assigns nine reasons for rejecting it as a fraud. But his last reason would have been sufficient, that it is not found in the early editions of Josephus. He also shows that the leader of the Jews (Josephus) could not call Jesus "the Christ," for that was the very thing the Jews denied. I have not room for all his reasons. He concludes by saying that "for these nine reasons it ought forever to be rejected as a forgery."

13. The reviewer calls " the code of Menu, of the Hindoos,' (he says Manu) 'a modern compilation.'" But the fourteen Christian authors which I have read on the subject consider it one of the oldest sacred books in the world. The Hindoo missionary, Allen, says it is 900 or 1,000 years old. He must settle the matter with his own witnesses.

14. He says, " Mr. Graves cannot affirm that the Jews bor-

rowed of the Persians." Yes, but I can affirm that a number of Christian writers say that they did not only borrow from the Persians, but of the Egyptians, and other nations. Mr. Enfield, Mr. Beers, Mr. Gibbon, Mr. Campbell, Mr. Cunningham, etc., etc., all make this affirmation. Here he has his own witnesses to overthrow again.

15. He says the legend appertaining to the Hindoo Buddha originated several centuries after Christianity was established. Here is another case of rebellion against all the historical authors and authorities I have ever read (not less than 27 in number), including the world-renowned Mr. Goodrich, the no less famous and pious Sir Wm. Jones, and that standard authority for the world, the New American Cyclopedia, and all the Christian missionary writers I have ever seen. They all place him from 300 to 1,000 years before Christ. I will give him into the hands of his own witnesses again, and he and they must fight it out.

16. He says the features of resemblance between Christianity and heathenism, on which I lay most stress, were stealings from the Apocryphal gospels. Well, I confess that is rich. The early Christians attributed the Apocryphal gospels to the devil. It seems, then, that the heathen obtained the doctrine of Christianity from the devil. And how did the devil come into possession of them? And when did he become a missionary for propagating the gospel, and what will be his reward for it?

17. The most important consideration in this discussion is

involved in the question, How did heathen nations come into possession of the doctrines of Christianity, as I have shown in my works that they teach and preach nearly them all? My learned and friendly reviewer attempts to account for it by assuming that soon after the establishment of Christianity, all the principal heathen nations underwent an entire change and revolution by the introduction of the doctrines and precepts of the gospel into their old, time-worn and musty systems. In noticing this position I will examine a little further the evidence he attempts to adduce to show that the Hindoos stole the whole history of Christ, and nearly all his religion in the sixth century, The assumption is based, as I have stated, upon the astrological calculations Mr. Bently, a man of some learning in some respects, but not much of an astronomer, though he wrote a work on the Hindoo astronomy. There is a long string of facts tending to show not only the absurdity but the impossibility of being any truth in this calculation, more of which I will cite. And to avoid extending my article, already longer than I intended, I will state them in the briefest manner possible, and leave the readers to their own conclusions.

1. The disciples of the Hindoo religions, including both Buddhism and Brahmanism, comprise about one-third of the inhabitants of the globe, and have been for nearly 2,000 years scattered all over the Eastern world, embracing India, China, Egypt, the Birman Empire, Tartary, Japan, Thibet, Ceylon, Siam, etc., etc. And it would appear, according to our reviewer and Mr.

Bently, that these 400 millions of heathens, with their old and musty systems of religion which had not been known to change essentially in a thousand years, suddenly, as by an electric shock, revolutionized and remodelled these old iron-bound systems of theology and mythology, one of them by stealing the life of Christ from the Aprocryphal gospels. and the other his doctrine and precepts and engrafting them into their antiquated time-worn creeds, though scattered as they were over the world for hundreds of thousands of miles with no telegraphs or railroads. and many of them no other way of learning for hundreds of years that a new system of religion had been introduced into the world. Those may believe this who can.

2. Had there been any real science or sense in Bently's theory, the discovery would have produced a sensation throughout the Christian world; but it was so manifestly weak and absurd that it attracted but little attention.

3. And it does not appear that any eminent astronomer, either in Europe or America, indorsed Bently's pretended discovery.

4. His own friends ridiculed his theory.

5. And finally a quietus was put upon the matter by some scholars a little smarter or sharper, and a little better posted, informing him that the same pointing of planets, his calculation was based on, took place prior to the time of Alexander, 330 B. C., which would indicate the time of Chrishna's birth to be (instead of 600 A. D.,) as long before Christ, as 300 millions of Hindoos

and all our able historians and the historical writers of other nations have always placed it. And thus he was compelled to give it up.

6. The Hindoos have always claimed that such star pointings are periodical, and hence had occured before.

7. The history of Hadrian, a Roman emperor, (who was born 76 A. D.,) proves that the name of Chrishna was known more than 500 years before the time Bently assigns for the origin of his story. He is also spoken of in the history of Alexander, 330 B. C. Perhaps my reviewer had better try to bring Alexander down into the Christian era.

8. None of the 150 Christian missionaries that I have heard of, who have been long operating in India, have indorsed Bently's theory, after examining their books, statues, temples, ancient languages, calculations in astronomy, &c., which furnish such convincing proof, that both those gods, Chrishna and Buddha Sakia, figured in their history more than 2,000 years ago.

9. And besides the 150 Christian missionaries, I have seen more than fifty authors, mostly Christians, who place Chrishna and Sakia, both before Christ. In fact, I have seen no reliable author who does not.

10. That profound Oriental scholar, Sir William Jones, in addition to the testimony of his, already, says: Asiat. Res. volume 1. "In the Sanscrit dictionary, compiled *more than 2,000 years ago*, we have the whole story of this incarnate god (Chrishna), reputedly

born of a virgin, and miraculously escaping in infancy from the tyrant ruler of the country, like Christ from Herod." Asiat. Res. volume 1, page 260.

11. The first Christian missionaries that entered India, which was long before Bently's planet pointing, found the history of both these gods *there*, and confessed their astonishment (as already stated) to find their histories and doctrines so near like those of Christ.

12. That standard authority, the New American Cyclopedia, places Buddha's birth at 543 B. C. (see volume 4, page 61). And Chrishna's birth, it admits, and all writers admit, was much earlier.

13. It says the history and doctrines of Buddha were introduced into China 65 B. C. And before that date, more than half of the doctrines of Christianity were taught in the old, long-established religion of the country. And yet Christian missionaries and everybody else admit that there has never been any perceptible change in the religion of China during the whole period of her existence, with respect to its principal doctrines. They possess not the slightest tendency to innovation. When, then, or how could she, or how did she, borrow the doctrines of Christianity?

14. And Egypt presents us with another formidable case. Not only had she the name of the Hindoo gods before the establishment of Christianity or the birth of Christ, but in her oldest system of religion are found taught nearly all the doctrines, both of

Judaism and Christianity, as shown in my books. And yet the proofs of the great age of her religion and its wide propagation long before Christ, are absolutely overwhelming and beyond refutation, and amply sufficient to convince any impartial investigation. Taylor says: "Everything of Christianity is of Egpytian origin." Egypt seems to have the most definite dates of her history, and the strongest proofs of the great antiquity of her religion and her government, of any other religion in the world. Her pyramids, her hieroglyphics and her dynasties of kings, are strong witnesses. Manetho furnishes us with a definite calculation of the reign of 300 kings, comprising 31 dynasties, and covering a period of 3,555 years extending down to 351 B. C., which the New American Cyclopedia says "is fully established by comparison with the monuments," (volume 7, page 36.) And under the reign of several of these kings, most of the doctrines of Christ and the whole code of the Jewish theocracy was taught. And all long before the advent of Christ, as shown in my two large works.

Why did not the reviewer attempt to overthrow my position with respect to the Egyptian Essenes, preaching and practicing nearly every doctrine of Christianity long anterior to the birth of Christ? "For it was here, (in Egypt), says Mosheim, the Essenes dwelt long before the coming of Christ," (vol. 1, p. 196); and I have given a long list of the most striking analogies in their doctrines and principles to those of Christ, to the *formidable number of sixty*, which embraces nearly all the doctrines and precepts of the gospel. I suppose the reason he skipped over this chapter, he found it impossible to bring down their origin into the Christian era. He has no Bently theory to help him out of this difficulty, hence, he barely alludes to the subject, and then dismisses it by saying: "No modern writer of eminence has confounded the Essenes with the Christians, except De Quincy, the opium eater." But here his historical knowledge falls short again. Bishop Marsh, Michaelis Weilting, a work entitled, "Christ the Spirit," and that world renowned Christian historian, Eusebius, (and others), all admit that the Essenes preached the doctrine of Christianity long before the coming of Christ. Eusebius makes the astounding statement that "those ancient Therapeuts (Essenes) were Christians, and their ancient writings were our gospels," (Eccl. Hist., p. 63). What have you to say to this, brother reviewer? And "Christ the Spirit," (by Hitchcock), says: "The Christians were the later Essenes—that is, the Essenes of the time of Eusebius, under a changed name, that name having been made at Antioch, where the disciples were first called Christians." Here is something definite and positive to prove that Christianity was preached before Christ. Let my reviewer then cease to call me an infidel, when I prove nearly all my positions by Christian writers. His judgment must be strongly biased to denounce or renounce such writers as DeQuincy. Hear what the world's authority, the New American Cyclopedia says about him. It says: "Mr. DeQuincy identified the Essenes as being the early Christians—that is, the early Christians were known as Essenes. *Such testimony coming from such a source is entitled to much weight,'"* (Vol. 1, p. 157). The Cyclopedia tells us DeQuincy's testimony is entitled to *much weight*. But the reviewer tries to create the impression that it is entitled to no weight at all. What confidence then can we repose in his judgment? He seems to assume DeQuincy could not tell the truth because he used opium. And, perhaps, the reviewer uses another narcotic, called tobacco. If so, must we assume he can't tell the truth? If either opium or tobacco can incapacitate men for telling the truth, then the world must be in a fearful and deplorable condition, indeed.

I will now assume that my main position is established beyond refutation, viz: that the doctrines of Christianity were preached in the world before the coming of Christ, which shows it to be of human origin, and whether taught by a dozen nations or only one nation, is of no consequence. One proves it as well as a hundred could do.

As my reviewer several times condemns my scholarship, and ranks me amongst the ignorant, because, as he assumes, I do not spell foreign names correctly, I will here "turn the tables," and show that it is only a case of "the pot calling the kettle black." There is scarcely a foreign name in his article but that he spells differently from that of some of our popular writers. I will cite a few cases in proof and illustration:

1. The Hindoo god, he spells Krishna; that profound Hindoo scholar, Sir William Jones, spells it as I do, Chrishna.—[See Asiat.

Res.] Renan spells it Christna; Dow spells it Chrishnoo; Spillard, Chreshnou, and others, Chreeshna, etc. 2. He speaks of Max Mueller, but there was no such a man, according to our standard cyclopædia. His name is Max Muller, as I stated before. 3. His Manu should be Menu, according to the same authority. 4. Sakyamouni should be Sakyamuni, according to the same authority, but most writers spell it as I do, Sakiamuni. 5. His Vishnu, Dow spells Vishnoo, and Robertson, Vishnou. 6. Buddha, Dow spells Boodha. 7. His Kali Yuga, Allen spells Kalee Yuya, and Child, Kali-Yug. 8. His Siva, Allen spells Sevu. 9. His Bahavet Gita, the Cyclopædia spells Baghavat Gita, and others Baghavat Geeta. 10. His Mahabarata, Allen spells Mahabarat. 11. His Puranas, the Cyclopædia spells Purans, and Dow, Poorans. 12. His Keliga should be Kaliga, according to most writers.

Here are a dozen cases besides some previously cited, and I could give other cases which prove that he has "become wise above what is written." And it suggests the conclusion that although he is well read in certain channels, he has not been over the whole field, and should have contented himself a while longer in being an humble student before he assumed the high position of a teacher and a critic, and calls others ignorant who had evidently read more than he has. Such a poor philologist can hardly be considered a trustworthy guide in matters of history.

I see by the last *Telegram*, that no less than four critics are now after me, which will perhaps justify me in extending my article a little longer than I intended. As they appear to be all friendly characters, I hope we can exchange thoughts in good feeling. As for Professor Swing, I have no criticism to offer upon his article.* It breathes the right spirit, and portrays quite beautifully the origin of the belief in Saviors. He traces it to the same origin "The World's Sixteen Saviors" does. He considers it as that work does, an outgrowth of man's moral and religious desires and aspirations. I confess the thought is beautiful, as well as apparently true. And a similar conception is involved in the belief of crucified gods. A work entitled, "The Progress of Religious Ideas," says the belief once generally prevailed that the gods would sometimes leave Paradise and descend to the earth on purpose to work, to suffer and to die for mankind. And thus becoming practically acquainted with the sorrows and temptations of humanity, they could justly judge its sins while they sympathized with its weakness and its suffering.— [Vol. 2, page 163.] And thus is suggested the origin of the belief in crucified gods. It seems rather beautiful, and contains a good moral, as is true of many other religious ideas and doctrines. And in this way the belief came to prevail extensively in the world, in different nations, that gods had suffered and died for mankind upon the cross. There appears to be but two well authenticated cases of actual crucifixion. Those two cases are Christ and Chrishna. The other cases are probably, most or all of them, mere figments of the imagination, or else borrowed from real cases. As to the belief or

*See Appendix.

conception, however, there can be no question. Suspensus crucis (suspended to the cross) found on monuments prove this. Professor Swing, doubtless, knows something of these facts of history.

I observe that the attention of the famous Henry Ward Beecher has been turned to our discussion. He suggests that the reviewer's article should be published as a "thin book." The word "thin" is quite suggestive, and I propose that it be entitled, "The Thin Book," as this title may indicate the character of its contents, and its logic and its conclusions, all of which are thin enough. And if the publisher will allow me to furnish one-half the contents of the work, I will furnish one-half of the funds for publishing it.

Another writer comes to the front with words of cheer for the reviewer, who signs himself "D." This is a very significant letter when applied to "the lower regions." His words are amusing, if not instructive. He frankly confesses he has never "wasted his precious time" in examining the books he condemns. If this be true, I suggest that his time must be worse than wasted now, when he writes on the subject. Such a man would not be allowed to sit on any jury, or testify before any Court of Justice in the civilized world — a man who prejudges a case and brings in a verdict before he has examined the evidence. Such a witness or juror would be ruled out of Court in three minutes. His decision in favor of the reviewer revives in memory the story of a young lady who hastened to the house of a neighbor at early dawn to see a new-born babe, Rushing to the cradle before the darkness of night was sufficiently dispelled to make objects clearly visible and discernible in the room, she exclaimed, "Dear me, what a beautiful babe—it is the very picture of its daddy!" But when a light was brought, it revealed the astonishing fact that there was no object in the cradle but an ebon cat. Mortified at her hasty decision, she confessed her mind was made up more from desire than from knowledge. Perhaps friend D's decision was controlled more by desire than knowledge. And when he comes to examine the case in broad daylight, he may find there is some cat about it. He will of course, accept this illustration in good feeling, as I cherish no feelings of unkindness towards him, if he does seek to bring odium on me by calling me an infidel; at least, he calls my books infidel works. And yet they have been read by hundreds of Christians and Christian clergymen. It has not been long since a popular Christian clergyman, residing in the same city in which my reviewer resides, called to see me, and stated he had purchased and read the work, and that he had but little objection to offer to it (The Sixteen Saviors). He stated he might differ some with respect to some conclusions, but the facts are undeniable, as they are mostly drawn from Christian authors. Such a man is "not far from the kingdom." My friend D. may call me an infidel, if he chooses, upon the assumption that I disbelieve the Bible, and yet I frankly confess that it contains moral lessons which, if he and other Christian professors would try as hard to live up to as I do, would save the world. Isaiah's beautiful and noble exhortation, " Come, and let us reason together," has often thrilled me with pleasure, and Paul's exhortation, "Try and prove all things," is noble. These two moral injunctions, if carried out in practice by everybody, would soon inaugurate that glorious era when truth, love and justice, and practical righteousness would cover the earth as waters cover the sea. But none of the Churches or Christian professors practice them, or else they would all meet and reason together, and the infidels with them, and compare their views and doctrines together in a spirit of friendship and loving kindness, to see who is right. I should be in favor of such a convocation as this. It would soon revolutionize the world, and establish universal harmony.

But I guess my friend D. has not faith enough in his Bible to try it. In this respect, I am a better Christian than he is, and have more faith in the power of truth, and am a better practical observer of the precepts of the Bible. The truth is, I do not condemn the Bible for what it may once have been, but for its present errors. That it contains errors now, thousands of Christian professors themselves admit. In fact, I hold no opinion or position but what is endorsed by many Christian professors. Why, then, am I called an infidel? I do not condemn the Bible, as such, but only the improper use to which it is applied. Nor will I condemn any man for his belief, as I have stated, if he will keep the doors and windows of his mind open for the admission of light. The error is in shutting out the light by refusing to investigate, and thus assuming we are infallible beings, like our friend D. I have made it a rule through life to give no decision on any controverted question until I hear all the parties, and thoroughly examine all the evidence. He who does not adopt this rule will find, at the end of the journey of life, that he has committed errors and mistakes. Mr. D. congratulates the reviewer on the successful refutation of the positions assumed in my books, although he has never read the books, and, consequently don't know what one of their positions is. This is about as sensible as the boy who claimed to be a great reader because his father was, although he had never seen inside of a book.

Nine distinct propositions are laid down in the first page of the Bible of Bibles, and twenty-one are laid down in the Sixteen Saviors, yet the reviewer has not so much as noticed any one of them. It is an easy matter to go through any book and select its weakest points for criticism, and leave its main positions untouched. Statements may be criticised and even proved false, and yet the leading positions and propositions of the book may remain intact and undisturbed. My rule is in criticising a book, to hunt for the strongholds and strong positions, and attack them first. The main object in all my writings is the development of truth. And I do most solemnly affirm before heaven and earth, that I would not propagate a single error to the world if I knew it. And I do solemnly declare, also, that I shall feel devoutly thankful to any person to point out errors in any of my writings if he or she can find any, and that is possible, as I do not claim to be infallible. I have no creed to support, no ism to maintain, and no church or society for whose reputation I am responsible. It is unreasonable, therefore, to suppose I am interested in the propagation of error, and should be denounced as a wicked or dangerous man. My way of meeting and answering slanderous reports is so to live that nobody who knows me will believe them or can believe them. I shall never fight nor sue for my character, not considering it worth such a sacrifice. And besides, such a remedy is worse than the disease.

And now I must have a word more with my reviewer as I see he has fired off another rocket in the last *Telegram*. Well, I like to discuss the question with him because he has "a reason for the hope that is in him." He is not so much accustomed to dealing in naked assertions without a show of proof, as most of those I have met have done. He seems to have a large store of facts, although they don't always prove what he assumes. He now comes forward with another witness to overthrow the assumed antiquity of the Hindoos, based on astronomical calculations. His witness is Mr. H. Klaproth, a German traveler, who figured in history about half a century ago. He studied the languages and acquired some knowledge of science, but never rose very high in the scale of literary fame. He fills about as short a chapter in history as the redoubtable Mr. Bently. The Cyclopedia honors them both with a brief notice, but it is very remarkable that it says not a word about either of their great astrological and astronomical discoveries which, if true, must have produced an entire revolution in the religious systems, not only of India, but of all the principal nations of the earth, and must have overthrown all the chronological tables and astronomical calculations for thousands of years.

The omission of the Cyclopedia to notice them is of itself entirely sufficient to bring discredit upon the whole story. And it is a remarkable circumstance that neither Mr. Bently, nor Mr. Klaproth furnish any reliable data or basis for their calculations. We must accept the little evidence they furnish and assume the balance, or be denounced as infidels. Mr. Klaproth asserts that the astronomical tables of India, running back for several thousand years, were constructed in the seventh century, A. D. But we are not furnished with the convincing evidence of this statement, but must assume that it is so and that he is infallible in his calculations. But Prof. Playfair, a philosopher of Edinburgh, furnishes us with some definite and positive facts calculated to overthrow Klaproth's calculations, or rather assumptions. Klaproth assumes that their astronomical calculations are back-handed, and were made since the events took place; but Prof. Playfair points to the fact that the calculations were made in a language so ancient that the present natives do not understand it, and with astronomical instruments cut or imbedded in solid rock bearing evidence of being several thousand years old. The natives know nothing about either the language or the instruments, while there is no important event in their history so late as the seventh century but what they are familiar with. Here is very strong presumptive evidence against the assumption of those astronomical calculations being of modern origin; and taken in connection with the fact that they have chronological tables showing the names and duration of time for the reign of each king for two thousand years, makes the case still stronger; and then when we look at the sculptures and inscriptions on their statues and temples, constituted of porphyry, the hardest rock in the world, we have a three-fold cord of evidence of their great antiquity that is hard to resist unless we have a creed at stake which is dearer to us than the truth.

I have now noticed nearly all the points and statements of any importance in the reviewer's article. I find one, however, near the close of his article which is of too serious a character to pass unnoticed as it seems to involve an indirect attack upon character. He says, "If the Bible be indeed such a nonsensical and immoral book as he contends, it is strange that none but men of loose doctrines if not of loose lives have discovered the fact." Here is a broad and not a very honorable insinuation against the character of a very numerous class of people comprising several millions, and, as I understand it, designed for me in particular. With respect to my own character, however; I have already spoken. I shall therefore notice its general application: and here permit me to remark, his historical knowledge seems to be sadly deficient again, and he virtually rejects and turns State's evidence against his own witnesses. Some of the leading religious journals, and some of the foremost writers in the ranks of the Christian church, contradict his statement in the most positive manner that the men and women of loose lives and character constitute the infidel class. Hear what that bigoted orthodox journal of world-wide fame, the New York Evangelist, says on this subject:

"To the shame of the church it must be confessed that the foremost men in all our philanthrophic movements in the interpretation of the spirit of the age, in the practical application of genuine Christianity, in the reformation of abuses in high and low places, in practically redressing wrongs, and in the moral and intellectual regeneration of the race, are the so-called infidels of our land. The church has pusillanimously left not only the working oar but the very reins of salutary reform to those she denounces as inimical to Christianity (infidels) and who are doing with all their might for humanity's sake what the church ought to do for Christ's sake, and if they succeed, *as succeed they will*, in banishing rum, restraining licentiousness, in reforming abuses, (among Christians), and in elevating the masses, then must the recoil upon Christianity be disastrous in the extreme. Woe, woe, woe, to Christianity when infidels * * get ahead of the church *in morals*, and in the practical work of Christianity. In some instances they are already far in advance. In the vindication of truth and righteousness they are pioneers, beckoning to a sluggish church to follow in the rear."

Here you have the testimony of one of your own witnesses in direct opposition to your own statement with respect to infidels being men of "loose lives and loose morals." You say they are, while this church organ assures us their morals are better than those of Christians and church members; which must we believe? And then that famous, pious and devout Christian writer, Catharine Beecher, comes forward with a long list of similar testimonies gathered from leading business men all over the country who are Christians, clergymen, bishops, etc., who testify in the most positive manner that infidels and outsiders in all parts of the country are superior in the exhibition of practical morality in all their dealings—that they are more honest, more reliable, and more truthful than Christian professors generally, and are thus practically superior in morals. Her statement and report are too long to present here. They may be found on page 319 of her "Appeal to the People." Our reviewer then must admit he is mistaken or else reject the testimony of his own witnesses. And it will be observed by the reader that in the more than fifty points he has raised against the books he criticises and their author, I have met him in nearly every case with his own witnesses. Therefore if my positions are wrong, and I am as bad a man as he represents, he will certainly admit this much, to say the least, that I am in pretty good company. His indirect charges of dishonesty and bad morals I accept in good spirit, believing they were made in haste and without due reflection, and that upon "sober second thought," he will see and admit he is mistaken. As for our discussion, allow me to say I cherish no fears but that the truth will ultimately prevail wherever it may be found, whether upon Christian or infidel ground. The great amount of interest which seems to be awakened in the minds of both the parties in this discussion will, I trust, result in the promotion of perfect good feeling in the minds of all interested. I will state in conclusion what I omitted to state in its proper place, that one of the oldest men in this county, residing near Richmond, (James Moore), who has read Gibbon, says he clearly understands this author by some of the language he uses, to imply that he believed the Essenes were the early Christians. If, then, Gibbon's language has been misquoted, his real sentiments have not been misrepresented, and not much harm is done by it.

KERSEY GRAVES.

NOTE.—I wish to add (a point before overlooked) that I am prepared to show that nearly all the strikingly similar doctrines of Chrishna and Christ (436 in number), were a part of the Hindoo religion long before the birth of Christ and the alleged forgeries on the Hindoo books Muller speaks of, and Muller himself would not deny it nor would he contend that the striking similarity between Chrishna and Christ, Sir William Jones points out in the Sanscrit Dictionary, were forgeries. And I wish also to state that Bently was a D. D., and his story died a hundred years ago and before he died, and has been seldom mentioned since.

MR. GRAVES' ADDENDA.

I have reproduced Mr. Graves' answer just as it was printed. In order that he may not be held responsible for any slips of the pen, and may have the full benefit of his sober second thoughts, I subjoin the following notes and explanations furnished by him to successive issues of the *Telegram* during the progress of the controversy.

[It may here be mentioned that the extract from Klaproth originally printed in a brief note containing some typographical corrections, has been inserted in its natural place in the present volume, and that two or three names wrongly spelled in the *Telegram*, have been corrected, thus depriving Mr. Graves' criticisms of the force they may have had when written]. J. T. P.

AN ERROR CORRECTED.

To the Editor of the Telegram:

In my article of last week, in speaking of the age of the code of Menu of the Hindoos, I am made to say, either by a blunder of my own or an error in the type-setter, that "the missionary Allen says, it is 900 or 1,000 years old." It should read, "the missionary Allen says, it is 900 or 1,000 years older than Christianity."

Allow me to say also, that I had intended to notice every point in my reviewer's article. But owing to the extreme length of my review, I omitted to notice a few points, which I considered of no importance. I still hold myself in readiness, however, to answer them, either in public or private, when called upon to do so, and answer any question appertaining to the subject of controversy.

KERSEY GRAVES.

It may perhaps be well for me to say with respect to the name Max Muller, that neither my reviewer's mode of spelling it, (Mueller,) nor mine, (Muller,) gives the true pronunciation of the word. The Germans place a bar over the "u" to denote the true sound.

Herod's decree was to destroy children under two years of age, instead of four, as stated in the review. Other typographical errors occur in the review, but are not deemed important.

K. G.

AN ERROR CORRECTED.

To the Editor of the Richmond Telegram:

Please be kind enough to allow me space sufficient to correct one more error. I have been so unmercifully pushed and over-tasked with writing of late that I have written with such haste, in some cases, as to commit mistakes, and also to overlook mistakes previously made. While writing my first large work I marked a large number of passages in different historical works, which, to save time, I got two persons to copy out for me. In some cases I find they copied too much, and in other cases not enough. One of the latter errors occurs in quoting from the New American Cyclopedia (vol. 7, p. 292), or was made by the type-setter.

When I wrote the review for the *Telegram*, as the Cyclopedia was not at hand, I copied the passage from an early edition of my book, in which the error occurs, without observing it was one of those errors I have corrected in later editions. (Here let me announce that I have a full list of corrected errors of both books, more than a hundred in number, which every person can see in print who may desire it). Both books are now revised and corrected. I have had a portion of the Cyclopedia for many years, but only recently the whole work came into my possession with the volume containing the error referred to.

The copyist makes the Cyclopedia say that DeQuincy identified the Essenes with the early Christians; and it appears he did according to the Cyclopedia. But the Cyclopedia says also that the Christians only assumed the name in disguise to save them from their enemies; (and some writers think they were never afterwards separated).

The Cyclopedia is made to say "such language coming from such a source is entitled to much weight." Here is a mistake. This should have been given as my language, instead of being included in the quotation from the Cyclopedia which I did not observe when I copied it for the *Telegram*. It will be seen I copied it word for word from my book, (page 218). For me to misquote the Encyclopedia, intentionally, would prove me to be the veriest fool, knowing that the reviewer has access to the work and would detect me in a moment. With this explanation the reviewer, if he should happen to find this error, is welcome to all he can make out of it, and all the other errors which are now corrected. Theodore Parker and Bayard Taylor both stated that they found errors in their works after they had passed through several editions. But these errors don't affect the main positions of the work.

I would like to furnish my reviewer with corrected copies of my works, and all persons having either of my works I will exchange with and furnish them a copy with the errors corrected.

Then criticisms will be in order and just, and not until then, unless confined to the leading positions of the work, which I am prepared to defend.

KERSEY GRAVES.

POSTSCRIPT.—Permit me to say to those who may read the reviewer's article this week, that I admit there are many errors in both of my works, which the reviewer possesses. But as I have explained how they occurred, and have stated they are not in the last editions, they will please make due allowance on this account. I desire to state that I admit that Max Muller speaks of some errors of Sir Wm. Jones in his " Chapter of accidents in comparative theology." But my statements of Muller's views of the Sanscrit dictionary is based on a declaration of his, made since that time. And my statement relative to "reliable authors" on the Herod massacre should be "reliable calculations." The Arru islanders spoken of as having no religion is a typographical error. It should be Arruba, as a portion of the natives of the Arru islands are Christian professors. Mr. Livingstone speaks of other tribes who have no religion.

K. G.

VALEDICTORY.

To the Editor of the Telegram:

Now as the discussion is closed, allow me to tender my thanks to J. T. P. for the able and gentlemanly manner in which he has reviewed my books. And you will be kind enough to allow me space sufficient for the explanation of a matter which I preceive is misunderstood, and without which explanation great injustice must be done to me, as well as to many of your readers. I have stated that more than a hundred typographical errors occurred in the first edition of "The World's Sixteen Crucified Saviors." But allow me to say they nearly all consisted in merely wrong letters or wrong words, such errors as could readily be detected by the reader, and therefore of no importance whatever. I believe that only two mistakes were made in quoting history that were not corrected *before the first edition went to press*—one from Gibbon, as noticed by J. T. P., and the other from the New American Cyclopedia, as noticed by myself, and these I am certain are not essential in settling any point, proposition or doctrine in the book. Most of the errors were corrected in the second edition; so that a recent examination satisfies me that not a dozen errors can be found in the edition now in the hands of my reviewer.

About thirty typograpical errors (as I have stated) occurred in the first edition of "The Bible of Bibles." Most of them consist in giving the wrong figures for verses and chapters in quotations from the Bible, while the quotations themselves are correct. Such or similar errors can be found in almost any book. I had supposed no reader could attach any importance to such errors. If any do, however, I will exchange with him or her, and furnish a corrected copy. As trifling as these errors are however, a criticism might be made on them that would give them undue importance. Hence I requested the kind editor to make no criticism on the first and uncorrected edition. With respect to the word Apis, allow me to say that while every person who ever saw the inside of an almanac knows that taurus is the generic Latin term for bull, apis is a Latin word and applied also symbolically to designate the Egyptian fabled bull. Apis is the Latin for bee (see Webster.) I will furnish a fuller explanation privately to any person desiring it. My note on apis made while reading the review of J. T. P. reads thus: "Apis, the Latin term for bee, used also symbolically to designate the Egyptian fabled bull." The statement, as criticised, is not as I intended it.

KERSEY GRAVES.

THE REPLY REVIEWED.

To the Editor of the Richmond Telegram:

RECAPITULATION.

You were kind enough to surrender a good deal of space to my exposure of the fallacies, mistakes and misrepresentations of Mr. Kersey Graves's two volumes, "The Sixteen Crucified Saviors" and "The Bible of Bibles." With your permission, I will more briefly examine Mr. Graves's very peculiar reply to my strictures. I cannot object to its length, for the author has been no more long-winded than myself. It would have been much more to the purpose, however, had he concentrated his attention on the chief points at issue, instead of dilating on minor features, quibbling over orthography, furnishing autobiographical details, and criticising matters not in controversy.

The real questions are, whether the idea of a virgin-born, miracle-working, and finally crucified Saviour entered into the conception of many nations of antiquity, and whether the one presenting most points of resemblance to Jesus Christ, viz: Krishna of India, was in the latest, and only coincident form of the myth, a pre- or post-Christian conception.

I showed that none of the classical authors, dictionaries of mythology and other authorities, had any thing to say of the crucifixion of fifteen of Mr. Graves's "Saviors." As to the sixteenth, Krishna, I quoted Burgess, Laplace, Bentley, and Klaproth, to prove that the Hindoo astronomy on which Mr. Higgins, Mr. Graves's chief authority, bases his claim of a very long series of cycles and avatars, is of late origin, and in its perfected form, post-Christian, as the famous treatise Surya Siddhanta certainly is. I also cited Wilson, the historian of Hindoo religion, to show that the Puranas in which alone is the story of Krishna in full bloom—the Vedas contain nothing of it and the epics only its germ—are not older than the eighth or ninth century of the Christian era, and the one specially devoted to Krishna latest of all. I showed that Mr. Higgins's Anacalypsis, while a work of great research, was absurd and superannuated in theory; and that M. Jacolliot, another author on whom Mr. Graves placed great dependence, was either a deceiver or deceived. I pointed out that while Buddha was a pre-Christian, historical character, the virgin-born Buddha of myth was described only in works which are post-Christian. If the stories are older, we can only suppose the fact. I adduced high authority for believing that the Zend Avesta, though a collection of much older prayers and hymns, dates its present compilation to a post-Christian period, and hence cannot have been the source from which any coincident Old Testament cosmogony was derived. I sketched the strong historical evidences of Christianity, quoted the assertion of the philosophical unbeliever, John Stuart Mill, that neither Jew nor Gentile could have invented the character of Christ, and glanced at the fact that men had always vaguely yearned for a deliverer, a point afterward developed with rare beauty and skill by Prof. Swing. I also exposed some glaring misrepresentations and many blunders.

MR. GRAVES ON MUELLER.

How has Mr. Graves met all these points? He is silent regarding Mill, and only endeavors to weaken Gieseler's partial acceptance of Josephus's testimony to Christ by saying that Lardner rejected the whole passage. The issue is between acute modern German scholarship and the historical knowledge of the middle of the last century; but the result is not of first class importance.

He says nothing of the Zend Avesta, and only mentions Buddha to convey the false impression that I regard all legend concerning him to be post-Christian. What I did say has been virtually repeated above. Mr. Graves has not any fault to find with the testimony of Laplace, Burgess, or Wilson. He is savage against Max Mueller for exposing Jacolliot, though he does not complain of equally emphatic condemnation by John Fiske. He goes so far as to sneer at Mueller as inferior in authority to the anonymous compiler of an article in a superseded edition of a Cyclopedia—(Mr. Graves uses the old American, of which the last volume was published in 1863, the new being eleven years later.) He is probably not aware that Mueller was commissioned by the East India Company to translate the Rig Veda; that his notes on the text are regarded as marking an era in the history of Sanscrit literature, and that no living man's dictum on Oriental theology and philosophy carries more weight. Mr. Graves's favorite Cyclopedia furnishes a biography of Mueller, but is silent regarding Mr. Higgins. This shows the compiler's estimate of the two men. In passing I must notice that Mr. Graves affirms that Mueller's name is Muller, and so appears in the Cyclopedia. I must contradict him. If he will look again, he will see two dots over the u, except in the capitals at the beginning of the notice. These dots, which can be used over a, o, or u, show that the letter is modified, or as the Germans say, becomes an umlaut. The change is the introduction of the e sound. Thus Müller is pronounced very like our word Miller, while Muller would be Mooler. It is allowable to add the e instead of using the dots, and the former course is taken where the fonts are not provided with the dotted letters. To close this discussion of Prof. Mueller's responsibility, which will seem wholly superfluous to those acquainted with the literature of the day, it may be said that he could not misrepresent Jacolliot without being exposed to rival philologists—for he has had his differences with one eminent man at least—and also that Col. Wilford has told the story of the frauds practiced on himself, in the pages of the Asiatic Researches.

THE TWO BENTLEYS.

But if Mr. Graves is angry with Mueller, he is furious against Bentley. That gentleman, in a communication to the sixth volume of the Asiastic Researches, showed by mathematical calculations, that, granting the position of the planets to have really been at the birth of Krishna as they are set down in his horoscope, he must have been born, if at all, A. D. 600. First, Mr. Graves styles Mr. Bentley "an arrogant, self-conceited, pedantic student of divinity, by the name of Richard Bently, (he erroneously omits the e) whom my critic calls an astronomer (God save the mark.") Next I am told that Mr. Bentley is "a man of some learning in some respects, but not much of an astronomer, though he wrote a work on the Hindoo astronomy;" a quietus having been finally put on him by other calculations giving Krishna greater antiquity. "The redoubtable Mr. Bently" is again mentioned, and lastly it is said that "Bently was a D. D., and his story died a hundred years ago and before he died, and has been seldom mentioned since."

Now, respecting these passionate but hardly reconcilable statements, I have only to say that Mr. Graves has mixed up two very different persons. Richard Bentley, a renowned theologian and Greek scholar, died in 1742, aged eighty. He probably never heard of Hindoo astronomy. John Bentley, a fellow of the Royal Asiatic Society, wrote the analysis of Krishna's horoscope, about the year 1801. The Edinburgh Review took up cudgels against him, and a sharp controversy followed. Bentley waged a gallant fight, and whether or not he established all the minutiæ of his conclusions, posterity has declared that he was right in general. Indeed, among his contemporaries, such men as the eminent French mathematician, Delambre, Dr. Maskelyne, Astronomer Royal of Great Britain, Cuvier, Heeren, and Klaproth, all sustained him. It is from Klaproth's letter to Bentley that I quoted the statement of the late origin of Hindoo astronomy. Mr. Graves thinks Klaproth a mere traveler. He was not a traveler except for the study of history and languages, and the contemptuous criticism is either an illustration of stupidity or a wretched shift to get rid of testimony which is not agreeable. I must not forget to add that all Mr. Graves's indignation against Bentley, and his blundering as well, are second-hand. The confusion of the theologian and the mathematician was first made in Taylor's Diegesis, and it is thence Mr Graves stole his thunder.

THE FACTS ABOUT INDIA.

While in matters of detail modern Orientalists may hold diverse opinions, there are certain great facts which are regarded as settled. Among these are the radical changes which affected the religious faith of the Hindoos after the Veda age. The Vedas, though of different periods, mainly inculcate nature worship, with occasional glimpses of one supreme being. Their gods generally have different names from those of the later Epic and Puranic periods and the trimurti or trinity, much less the Krishna incarnation, are not found in them or in the laws of Manu, a later production than the Vedas—not a *late* one as was erroneously printed in my last. There is almost no reliable Indian history. Only one date before Christ has been actually verified; that of a king named Chandrugupta, who ascended the throne B. C. 315. The authentic history of India begins with the twelfth century of our era. Hence a thorough comparison of languages and dialects, and a careful collation of the manuscripts containing the sacred writings have been required. This has been the work of years, but largely of the last quarter of a century. It is made clear that the elaborate Brahmanical ceremonial gradually superseded the Vedaic nature worship; that a war ensued between the priestly and soldierly castes; that the former being victorious by the aid of the common people, intermingled some of their superstitions with their own; that the trinity and incarnations were elaborated by slow degrees, and became more definite when the rise of the opposing faith of Buddhism rendered a firm stand necessary, reaching their full height only when Buddhism was finally expelled from the Indian peninsula twelve or fourteen centuries after the Christian era. I substantiated these general facts in my former article, but I will make a few additional citations to clinch the argument.

Chambers's Encyclopædia, a work noted for its impartiality and its avoidance of all disputed positions, and anything which looks like partisanship, says of the great epics:

> "Krishna has in the Bhagavad-gita the rank of the supreme deity, but there are other passages, again in the Mahabharata, in which the same claim of Siva is admitted, and an attempt is made at comparing their rival claims by declaring both deities one and the same. Sometimes, moreover, Krishna is in this epos declared to represent merely a very small portion of Vishnu. In the Mahabharata, therefore, which is silent also regarding many adventures in Krishna's life, fully detailed in the Puranas, the worship of Vishnu in this incarnation was by no means so generally admitted or settled as it is in many Puranas of the Vishnuit sect, nor was there at the epic period that consistency in the conception of a Krishna avatar, which is traceable in the later works."

I quoted the opinion of Wilson, the learned writer on the religion of the Hindoos, that the Puranas are not anterior to the eighth or ninth centuries, (of the Christian era,) and the most recent not above three or four centuries old. Mr. Graves has nothing to say to this, except to produce the loosely expressed opinion of Sir William Jones. Sir William was a great and learned men, but he died in 1794. Since his day Oriental research has made prodigious strides. One might as well quote him on questions of philology and ethnology against Mueller, Weber, Lassen, Burnouf, and other modern scholars, as to depend on Captain Tuckey, who reached the lower falls of the Congo, in 1816, and there died, as authority regarding the upper river, now that we have Stanley's narrative to read.

Weber and Lassen, German authorities of the first-class, and not known as religious enthusiasts, agree on the interpretation of a passage of the Mahabharata: That it shows that at an early period of the history of the Christian church, three Brahmans visited some community of Christians, either in Alexandria, Asia Minor or Parthia, and that on their return they were enabled to introduce important changes in their hereditary creed, and more especially to make the worship of Krishna the most important feature of their system. At this time, though India was pretty well known to the Christian world, there was no confounding of Christians with Brahmans. The famous Tertullian said: "We are no Brachmans, nor Indian gymnosophists, dwellers in woods, estranged from the affairs of life. We know that our duty is to give thanks for everything to God, the Lord and the Creator." Yet there was intercourse between the East and West.

Weber has seen in the Hindoo Kali-yuga when the tenth avatar of Vishnu is to occur, a borrowing from the white horse of Revelation. He doubts whether the incarnated Krishna was identical with the Indian Hercules of the Greek writers, "who was no incarnation, in the proper sense of the language, and very different from the Krishna of later times." Mr. Pavie, a prominent French Orientalist, says in the preface to a translation of a Purana, published in 1852:

"Krishna worship is the most recent of all the philosophical and religious systems which have divided India into rival sects. Based on the theory of successive incarnations, which neither the Veda nor the law-makers of the first Brahmanic epoch admit, Krishnaism differs in all points from the creeds peculiar to India: so that one is inclined to regard it as a borrowing, made from foreign philosophies and religions."

It is certain that the epics have been greatly interpolated; less than a quarter of the Mahabharata, for example, having entered into its original composition. That the Bhagavat-gita, the episode in which Krishna appears in divine, but not in the later semi-Christian garb, is post-Christian; that the apocryphal Gospel of the Infancy was circulated at an early period on the Malabar coast, and was held in special honor by the Manichean heretics, who strove to corrupt Christianity with Indian theories. According to Eusebius, the Christian missionary, Pantaenus, went as far as India. Flourishing Christian churches were established in the Hindostan as early as the latter part of the second century. These are well established facts, and show that the Hindoos had abundant opportunity for investing one of their favorite deities with new attributes. Yet, how different is Christianity from Krishnaism. The one protects purity and proclaims the sacredness of human life; the other abounds in licentious rites, and in the month of July celebrates the departure of Krishna from his native land in the horrible festival of Juggernaut! Yet, the faiths are essentially the same, according to Mr. Graves.

MR. GRAVES'S REMARKABLE AUTHORITIES.

But he has authorities who bear testimony to facts otherwise unattainable. I shall not trouble myself about his eminent Mr. Goodrich, whom I guess to be no other than the well known compiler, "Peter Parley," and Horace Greeley, who knew as much about Sanscrit as he did about Greek, but quote the following paragraph from his reply:

"The secret of the whole matter is: two very popular and learned authors, who have investigated and studied the subject more critically than any other writers who ever wrote on the subject, claim to be able to throw new light on the subject. They claim, just as Max Muller does, with respect to the Hindoo Vedas, to have discovered that changes and alterations or omissions were made many years ago in the histories of the oriental gods, by which some of the most important events of their lives were either left out or materially altered. Those two authors are Alexander Dow and Sir Godfrey Higgins. (All the English writers I have seen, prefix Sir to his name, my critic to the contrary notwithstanding.)"

To begin with a point of little importance, I must repeat that Mr. Higgins is not called "Sir." If Mr. Graves will look into his favorite Diegesis he will see him mentioned as "Godfrey Higgins, Esq., of Skellow Grange." Next he evidently quotes Dow at second hand. Alexander Dow, who died in 1779, translated from the Persian of Ferishta, a History of India, which has no bearing on religious traditions. This was published between 1768 and 1772, when very little was known respecting the Oriental religions. In an introduction of seventy-six pages, Col. Dow gives a very superficial sketch of Brahmanism, much inferior in every way to a modern Encyclopædia article. He mentions, I believe, that the Brahmans accused the Jews and Mohammedans of having borrowed some religious rites, and that is about all.

MR. HIGGINS AND HIS WEAKNESSES.

As for Mr. Higgins, I find quoted in Allibone's Dictionary of Authors, a work of standard authority, the following comment on the Anacalypsis, from the London Athenaeum, a leading literary weekly of that metropolis, which fully confirms my estimate of the book in my former communication:

"It occasionally happens that books written to display some peculiarity of system, or,—as the wicked say,—crotchet of the author, turn out to have a value of their own, from the very great number of well indexed and well referenced facts which they contain. We remember being much struck by seeing among the books of reference in the Museum Reading Room, the Anacalypsis of Godfrey Higgins. Never was there more wildness of speculation than in the attempt to lift the veil of Isis. But thousands of statements cited from all quarters, and very well indexed, apparently brought the book into such demand as made it convenient that it should be in the reading room itself."

This was published in August, 1856, more than twenty years ago. The book is to be found in many of the large libraries of Europe and this country, yet we see no really learned skeptics on either side of the water urging its theories against Christianity. Mr. Higgins was about the last of the host which fought the faith under the banners of Orientalism.

Mr. Graves quotes a silly story from Higgins, relative to the concealment of some Hindoo manuscripts, which told against Christianity, by a bishop. It is impossible that any prelate could suppress all of the many manuscripts kept with such religious care by the natives; or secure the co-operation of the Brahmanical opponents of the Bible in keeping such statements quiet. Moreover, from the first entrance of the English into India, unbelievers were proclaiming the evidences which its religion afforded against the Christian faith. They failed to produce many, and have been beaten out of these. As we have said, Mr. Higgins was one of the last of his class, and Mr. Graves has attempted to reanimate a corpse.

He also quotes Moor's Pantheon, an interesting but antiquated work, published in 1810, which he says contains the portrait of "The Crucified Chrishna." Mr. Moor is of a different opinion. He says:

> "The subject is evidently the crucifixion; and by the style of workmanship, is clearly of European origin, as is found also by its being in duplicate. These crucifixes have been introduced into India, I suppose, by Christian mis-

sionaries. They are well executed, and in respect to anatomical accuracy and expression, superior to any I have seen of Hindoo workmanship."

I have the picture before me as I write, and in spite of Mr. Higgins's attempt to prove that Moor was wrong, and Mr. Graves's exaggerated endorsement of Mr. Higgins, must agree with the author. This picture was one of two brought to Mr. Moor by a native, but Mr. Higgins says that the book contains others, copied from the rock temples, that abound in India. These he holds to be of great antiquity. On the contrary, these temples are of Buddhist construction, and therefore comparatively late; that at Elephanta, near Bombay, being ascribed to the fifth century after Christ. They afford no support to the pre-Christian Krishna theory.

In this connection, and before dismissing Mr. Higgins, I may remark that Mr. Graves quotes him as alleging that the current versions of the sufferings of Prometheus are garbled, and that he was crucified. It is enough to say that the ancient Greek poet, Hesiod, says that Prometheus was liberated by Hercules; and that Æschylus represents that the Centaur Cheiron, was mortally wounded by Hercules, and sent to Prometheus's place in Tartarus. There are other variations in these two narratives, and there are still other versions, but in none of them does the crucifixion come in. Mr. Higgins's word is of no weight against the classical writers, who, of course, had no Christian prejudices to gratify.

THE ESSENES.

Having disposed of the general issue, and shown that Mr. Graves has not shaken a single vital position, but has only proved himself more ignorant than I thought him, I pass to the Essenes. He is evidently much fluttered about the misquotation of Gibbon's note, and promises a correction. A little later he takes courage from the assurance of a certain citizen of Richmond that he is correct in his belief that Gibbon agrees with him. Were this true it would not justify the garbling of a passage, and he will derive no comfort from the text to which the note refers. That text says of the reception of Christianity at Alexandria, "It was at first embraced by great numbers of the Therapeutæ or Essenians of the Lake Mareotis, a Jewish sect which had abated much of its reverence for the Mosaic ceremonies. The austere life of the Essenians, their fasts and excommunications, the community of goods, the law of celibacy, their zeal for martyrdom, and the warmth—though not purity—of their faith, already offered a very lively image of the primitive discipline."

This, coupled with the declaration of the note that Basnage has "demonstrated in spite of Eusebius and a crowd of modern Catholics that the Therapeutae were neither Christians nor monks," is in accordance with the latest views, drawn from the Talmuds and other ancient Jewish writings, which correct the impressions based on Philo and Josephus—Eusebius being a mere copyist of the former, who lived two hundred years before him.

The Essenes were Pharisees of the Pharisees; men who held most exaggerated notions of the Mosaic ritual, and were divided into degrees or castes.

The Therapeutae were of the same stock as the Essenes of Judea, but clung more lightly to the law, and were affected by the Greek philosophy, especially the Pythagorean, so widely diffused in Egypt. Both practiced, however, elaborate washings, and other rites.

They mainly resembled the Christians in the points in which the latter resembled their Jewish brethren, and Mr. Graves's sixty points of coincidence cannot stand against the testimony of history, and the reproofs by the Apostle Paul of the Galatians for keeping days, etc., the censure of those who forbade marriage, and the general spirit of the New Testament. Undoubtedly Essenism, like other Jewish theories, influenced the early church, but it was not identical with it.

MR. GRAVES'S ORIGINAL QUOTATION.

I said that no modern writer of eminence except Thomas De Quincey identifies the Essenes and the Christians, but Mr. Graves is determined to make the most of him. We quote:

> "Hear what the world's authority, the New American Cyclopedia, says about him (DeQuincey). It says, 'Mr. DeQuincey (Mr. Graves spells the word De Quincy) identified the Essenes as being the early Christians. That is the early Christians were known as Essenes. *Such testimony coming from such a source is entitled to much weight.*'

The words which I have put in these single quotation marks, since they are included in a citation from Mr. Graves, are credited by him to volume 1, of the Cyclopedia. This is a mistake, but it is of little consequence, since the work is ranged alphabetically. But the Cyclopedia says something quite different—here it is:

"De Quincey has sought to identify them (the Essenes) with the early Christians, who, surrounded by dangers, assumed the name and mode of life of the Essenes as a disguise."

There is not a word about the testimony being of much weight, and I supposed your compositor might have included in quotation marks what was only added by Mr. Graves, but further reading does not allow this explanation. Either Mr. Graves has been deceived by some unscrupulous writer from whom he took these quotations at second-hand, or he has been guilty of a contemptible forgery. He adds: "The Cyclopedia tells us De Quincy's testimony is entitled to much credit." Abstinence from tobacco and stimulants does not always insure truthfulness. I begin to think that his misrepresentation of Gibbon was not so purely accidental. Even if it were, there is not the same palliation, for Mr. Graves expressly says he owns the Cyclopedia, and, if so, he certainly ought to have looked for himself.

Then we are not satisfied with his explanation of his slander against the Apostle Paul. The verse he did not quote *is* a part of the statement. In the Greek original, which is not divided into verses, the connective *kai* (and) has a small letter at the beginning.

Besides in the verse he did not cite, the apostle indignantly repudiates the doing evil that good may come. Does this not include lying for the alleged glory of God? If Mr. Graves has the least particle of honesty he will expunge from his volumes this several times reiterated falsehood.

IRENAEUS DISAPPOINTS MR. GRAVES.

Having grossly libeled an apostle, we cannot expect that Mr. Graves should be very careful to avoid misrepresenting a father of the church. He says that Irenaeus, whose name he spells Ireneus, denies that Christ was crucified. "This learned and pious bishop," he says, "declared upon the authority of the martyr Polycarp, who claimed to have got it from St. John and the elders of Asia, that Christ was not crucified, but lived to the age of fifty." This is "important if true," for Irenaeus was the great opponent of the heresies of the day. But it is, at least, one-half false. He believed that Christ lived until fifty, from an erroneous interpretation of the words of the Jews (John viii. 57), "Thou art not yet fifty years old, and hast thou seen Abraham?" He argued that as Christ bore the sins of all men, He must have had a personal experience of all the ages of human life. Yet no one held more fully than he to the reality of his Master's death, and that on the cross. I quote from his treatise against the Heretics:

"They [the heretics] maintain that the Lord, too, performed such works simply in appearance. We shall refer them to the prophetical writings and prove from them both that all things were thus predicted regarding Him, and did take place undoubtedly, and that he is the only son of God. And what shall I more say? It is not possible to name the number of the gifts which the church [scattered] throughout the whole world has received from God in the name of Jesus Christ, who was crucified under Pontius Pilate, and which she exerts day by day for the benefit of the Gentiles."

I think Mr. Graves has had enough of the testimony of Irenaeus.

HOW MR. GRAVES TREATS THE BIBLE.

As a critic of the Bible Mr. Graves is decidedly and disreputably original. He is so bitter against it, that he accepts every wild story that may serve his purpose; finds difficulties and contradictions where no one else has espied them, and hence obscures the real points of which shrewd unbelievers have availed themselves. There are questions of interpretation yet to be settled; passages the harmonizing of which is not easy, if possible. Yet they do not affect the general truthfulness of the work, render any doctrine doubtful, or do more than disappoint human curiosity. The Bible is translated into plain old Saxon English. There are words used which time has rendered coarse. Offenses are described about which people do not talk in good society. They are never, however, described to gratify prurient desires or a debased taste, but recorded as matters of fact and warning, just as they enter into secular history or into the records of a legal tribunal. The existence of such facts and crimes cannot be ignored. We all know of them, and a book which guides men's conduct must notice them. If there is any complaint to make it solely relates to the translation, and a modernized one is now in preparation. The Bible describes the gross misconduct of some men, whom, on the whole, it pronounces good. They are to be judged by the standard of their day, not of ours, and the candor of the statements is strong proof of the truth of the narrative. If the Old Testament tells what was done by the Patriarchs or Israelites, it does not necessarily justify their acts, even when it fails to reprobate them. The deeds are often suffered to speak for themselves.

Mr. Graves is indignant that I should say he denounces the Bible, and quotes two or three passages from his volumes, in which he says the Bible contains "much that is beautiful in thought and expression;" again, that "there is scarcely a book or even a chapter in the whole Bible that does not evince a spirit of religious devotion, and an effort for the right; and the prophets often breathed forth a spirit of the most elevated poetry." Still further, he says, "the Bible is a very useful book in its place," and he has "no objection to urge against the Bible, but only to the improper use to which it is applied." This is all very well, but is hardly consistent with other and much more forcibly urged declarations.

In his list of the Leading Positions of his "Bibles," he explains the alleged existence of several thousand errors in the Christian Bible, by saying that "it originated at a period when the moral and religious feelings of the nation which produced it co-operated with the animal propensities instead of an enlightened intellect.

Again, he says, "as the Christian Bible is shown in this work to inculcate bad morals, and to sanction, apparently, every species of crime prevalent in society in the age in which it was written, the language of remonstrance is frequently employed against placing such a book in the hands of the heathen, or the children of Christian countries, and more especially against making the Bible the foundation of our laws, and the supreme rule of our conduct." In the body of the work these ideas are developed at length.

Two hundred alleged instances of obscene statements in the Bible are cited in figures; the Jehovah of the Bible is set down as an angry, malevolent being, unworthy of reverence. The mere reading of the history of Moses, it is held, will weaken the natural and instinctive love of honesty, justice and morality, unless he is strongly fortified by nature against moral corruption. The patriarchs and prophets are handled far from gently. Under distinct heads, we are told that the Bible sanctions murder, theft, war, intemperance, slave-holding, polygamy, licentiousness, wife-catching, assassination, and so on.

Finally, to sum up, though I have not nearly exhausted the catalogue of complaints, Mr. Graves says, "we see not how to escape the conviction that the Bible has inflicted, and must necessarily inflict, a demoralizing influence on society, where it is read and *believed*. It is morally impossible for *any person* to read and believe a book sanctioning, or appearing to sanction, so many species of crime and immorality without sustaining more or less moral and mental injury by it." The italics are Mr. Graves's. I will leave the reader to decide whether he is a practical believer in the doctrine that consistency is the vice of ignoble minds, or whether, knowing the Bible to be so atrocious a book, he has in two or three places highly recommended it.

ALLEGED CONTRADICTIONS, ETC.

It would be amusing were it not sad and revolting to see how every verse and clause is twisted and tortured to make out a contradiction or an absurdity. I will give a few specimens:

"As Eve was pronounced 'the mother of all living,' when they were no human beings in existence, but she and Adam, the inference seems to be that she was the mother of herself, her husband and all the animal tribes." As if her prospective place of mother of all human beings, was not the obvious meaning. An impostor would not have been guilty of the stupidity which Mr. Graves imagines; an idiot could not have written the narrative in which it appears. "Methuselah's time was not out till ten months after the flood began, according to Bible chronology. Where was he during these ten months?" As if the book of Genesis recorded the month of the great antediluvian's birth.

There are no end of "scientific" objections to the biblical narratives of the creation and deluge, which are wonders of malignant absurdity. Mr. Graves knows as much of natural science as he does of Oriental literature, and that is merely to seize on whatever he thinks will tell, caring not at all whether it be true or false. Thus he finds a "contradiction" between the threat to Adam that in the day thou eatest thereof thou shalt die and his subsequent long life, as if it were sure that the "death" threatened meant physical dissolution. There is a contradiction between the sensible proverbs that advise the answering of a fool according to his folly on some occasions and not answering him on others; injunctions, both of which are constantly put in practice by sensible people. There is contradiction between the different uses of the word tempted, in its literal sense and in that of trial. There is a contradiction between Christ's command to the disciples to baptize all nations, and Paul's statement that his special duty was not to baptize but to preach.

It is useless to multiply the citations of these quibbles. They reflect no credit on Mr. Graves, or rather on the pamphlet from which he has borrowed most or all of them, and which, as I have before said, has been thoroughly exposed and answered by Mr. Haley. I have given enough examples to show the precious stuff of which the "Bible of Bibles" is composed.

THE MASSACRE OF THE INNOCENTS.

My critic does not like my computing the children destroyed by Herod, at a dozen. He never heard of such a small number.

Yet the tradition reckoning them by thousands, is a senseless legend of the Greek church. Bethlehem was a small village, and the number of male children under two years, not four as Mr. Graves has it, in it and its vicinity, which is the meaning of "coasts," obsolete in this sense, would be a fair number. Let Mr. Graves reckon from some little Indiana hamlet. I have good authority for this conclusion, viz: Smith's Bible Dictionary unabridged edition, a very scholarly work. Moreover, I have that which may suit Mr. Graves better, the testimony of the American Cyclopedia, under the title Herod. It says:

"The event (the massacre) is recorded only by one evangelist (Matthew ii, 16), and being confined to the neighborhood of a single village, may naturally have passed unnoticed by Josephus amid the many more general atrocities of his (Herod's) government."

CHRISTMAS.

This will do for the massacre of the innocents. As for the selection of the twenty-fifth of December as Christmas day, it is of very little consequence whether the actual date of Christ's birth is taken or not, since the fact must be matter of speculation. The church did not agree upon the matter until the fourth century. Sir Isaac Newton held the opinion that the winter solstice was chosen because most of the feasts, for which there is no direct New Testament authority, were originally fixed at cardinal points of the year —as other feasts had been before them—and that the first Christian calendars having been so arranged by mathematicians at pleasure, without any ground in tradition, the Christians afterwards took up what they found in the calendars; so long as a fixed time of commemoration was solemnly appointed they were content. It is the spirit of the commemoration, not chronological exactness, that is important. It is of no possible consequence whether the Mithraic festival or the Roman Saturnalia coincided in time or not.

SOME BIG AND LITTLE BLUNDERS.

There are some minor topics I must briefly notice, for Mr. Graves has rampaged over the whole theological and historical field, in search of weapons to assail me. He has for the most part picked up boomerangs which have recoiled on himself. For example, he says he knows that Apis was not a savior properly so-called, for he learned when a boy that Apis was the Latin for a bull. I have always thought that Taurus was the word, while Apis is a modification of Hapi, or the hidden. After this specimen of Egyptological lore it is not surprising to be told that "most of the doctrines of Christ and the whole code of the Jewish theocracy was taught" on the banks of the Nile. I do not know whether most to admire the author's information or grammar. (See Note.)

NOTE.—In this letter as originally published, I contented myself in the assertion of a well known fact. Were Mr. Graves right, he would find himself in the dilemma of claiming that the religions of Egypt and India were identical, since he maintains that they are both reproduced in Christianity. Lest, however, I may seem to regard my own authority as sufficient, I will quote from James Freemans Clarke's "Ten Great Religions," an interesting, valuable, and not rigidly orthodox work, a passage which concisely sets forth what other authorities maintain more in detail:

"Of Egyptian theology proper, on the doctrines of the gods, we find no traces in the Pentateuch. Instead of the three orders of deities we have Jehovah; instead of the images and pictures of the gods we have a rigid prohibition of idolatry; instead of Osiris and Isis, we have a Deity above all worlds and behind all time, with no history, no adventures, no earthly life.* * His (Moses') severe monotheism was very different from the minute characterization of Gods in the Egyptian Pantheon. * * Nothing of the popular myth of Osiris, Isis, Horus and Typhon is found in the Pentateuch; nothing of the transmigration of souls, nothing of the worship of animals, nothing of the future life and judgment to come, nothing of the embalming of the bodies and ornamenting of tombs. The cherubim among the Jews may resemble the Egyptian sphinx; the priests' dress in both are of white linen; the urim and thummim, symbolic jewels of the priests are in both; a quasi hereditary priesthood is in each, and both have a temple worship. But here the parallels cease. Moses left behind Egyptian theology, and took only some hints for his ritual from the Nile. There may perhaps be a single exception to this statement. According to Brugsch and other writers, the papyrus interred with the mummy contained the doctrine of the divine unity. The name of God was not given, but instead the words Nuk Pu Nuk—"I am the I am." If this be so the coincidence is certainly very striking."

To this we may add that the discordance was equally startling. Moses taught God's unity to all, while monotheism was a secret doctrine in Egypt; the grossest idolatry being permitted and even encouraged among the masses. It is a fact, not very consoling to those who hold that religion, like everything else, passes by evolution from lower to higher forms, that the ancient primitive faith of Egypt, like that of Chaldea, Phoenicia and Syria, was monotheistic. M. de Rouge, after quoting various early Egyptian attestations of the divine unity, asks:

"Were these noble doctrines the product of ages? Assuredly not, for they existed more than two thousand years before the Christian era. On the contrary, polytheism of which we have pointed out the sources, developed and progressed without interruption to the times of the Ptolemies. More than five thousand years ago the hymns to the unity of God originated in the valley of the Nile * * and we see in the later period Egypt sunk in the most frightful polytheism."

M. Mariette in his account of the Museum of Boulac, after bearing equally strong witness to the original monotheism of the Egyptians, adds: "But Egypt did not know how to remain on this sublime height." While Egypt and the other countries with which the Jews maintained intercourse, yielded completely to the idolatrious spirit, the less polished Israelites, after many backslidings finally became thoroughly monotheistic. Why did they succeed where their more refined neighbors failed? Why, we may further say, were they the only nation of antiquity to conquer the tendency to polytheism? The answer must be found in the system they were taught, not in any moral or intellectual virtue of their own. We may add that Mr. Graves finally discovers that Apis is the Latin for bee, and not for bull, but this has nothing to do with the Egyptian divinity.

Again he tells us that " the history of Hadrian, a Roman emperor (who was born 76 A. D.), proves that the name of Chrishna was known more than 500 years before the time Bentley assigns for the story." As Bentley's date was A. D., 600, it would make Krishna a contemporary of Hadrian, and so post-christian. But Mr. Graves confounds Hadrian with the historian Arrian, his contemporary, to whose mention of Alexander's knowledge of an Indian hero named Krishna—not the incarnation—I referred in my last article. I have not yet discovered a Bermuda in Burmah, nor how Ixion's punishment in hell could be the crucifixion of a savior, and do not object to the printing of "Col." for Cardinal being alleged a mistake to the typographer. The ignorance showed itself in the declaration that "Col." or Cardinal Wiseman was "ten years a missionary in India." He claims to have discovered in his Cyclopedia the identity of Eros, the God of Love, and Esus or Hesus, the warlike divinity of the Druids. This is untrue. The Cyclopedia only describes Eros as the Greek equivalent of the Latin Cupid.

As for Robert Taylor, I did not affirm that he "repented." I am afraid he never did. I said he "recanted," and he did this at least twice. In early life, after deserting the pulpit, and finding infidelity did not pay, he published an humble confession in Latin in the London Times, which his own brother affirmed was inspired by mercenary considerations. Later he was known as the "Devil's Preacher," and later still, I quote from recollection a brief sketch, written, I think, by the late G. Vale, he quarreled with Richard Carlile, declined to be called reverend any longer, and after marrying, became a physician. The account referred to, says he died in

France in 1848. If my memory does not fail me this is a mistake, for 1843, in which year Dodsley's Annual Register records his death. I was told on high authority that his career as a "Christian," which he claimed to be after his marriage, was by no means creditable, and that he was a victim of intemperance.

I can see no difficulty in reconciling the Pauline statement that Christ was seen by five hundred disciples at once, with that of Acts that one hundred and twenty believers were gathered about the eleven at the time a successor to Judas was elected. If Roman Catholic missionaries were surprised at the parallelism of their religious uses to those of the East when they visited it, in the sixteenth and seventeenth centuries, this does not involve the fact that those similarities had existed for countless ages. The Nestorians sent priests all through India and China before the seventh century of the Christian era. As for the spelling of Eastern words, there are various systems, to no one of which I have rigidly adhered. I only object to the attempt to make capital for a theory by approximating the word Krishna to Christ.

I believe I have now noticed not only the main features of Mr Graves's paper but his most trifling quibbles; with the exception of allegation that a crucifix fastened to an Irish round tower is of Oriental origin, solely because there are two animals at its feet, one supposed to be a sheep, the other an elephant. I have the picture, but the elephant is not there, It is a nondescript beast, most like a tapir, but really to be certainly identified with no living thing. I should decide there was perhaps more artistic stupidity than Oriental influence here.

CONCLUSION.

I must now leave Mr. Graves and his books. I have not quoted the ribaldry the latter contain respecting the incarnation and other subjects deemed specially sacred by Christians, nor have I examined the "criticisms" of the Scriptures with elaborate minuteness." The task would be endless, for the volumes are tissues of misrepresentations from beginning to end; sometimes stupid, and always bitter. Many, I might say most, are so weak that they refute themselves and there are none which cannot be found answered in works accessible to nearly all. My purpose has been to strike deeper; I have destroyed the foundation on which the pretentious superstructure has been erected.

I have shown that all the "coincidences," save those which the constitution of the human mind makes a part of all religions, are post-Christian; and that there has been no borrowing or imposition on the part of the church. I have shown also that Mr. Graves is incompetent to decide between authorities, and blundering and dishonest in those he uses. He may be a good neighbor and an honest man in his daily walk. He declares himself such, and I have no reason to disbelieve him. But he is the exact reverse in controversey. He is mentally and morally jaundiced. I do not wish to be severe or use rough words. Yet, if a quack, who should kill people by the reckless administration of drugs, of whose nature he is uninformed, should be held to strict account, is not a man culpable who endeavors to settle questions that concern man's immortal destiny while ignorant of the evidences of the doctrines he pretends to teach? I have no right to call in question Mr. Graves's sincerity, yet I trust I have convinced him that he had better study other books than those of Higgins and Taylor, before publishing more volumes, and that those already in print, need much in the way of excision and modification. If he will study with a desire to learn the truth, not to make an argument, he may get new light, and change his position, much to his good. This I sincerely hope he may do.

J. T. P.

Cincinnati, February 22, 1879.

POSTSCRIPT.

Where there are two legitimate ways of reaching the same end, it often happens that neither has a monopoly of advantages. By reproducing my letters on Mr. Graves's works essentially as they were first published, I have escaped the possible dullness of abstract disquisition. Moreover, by leaving him to be his own advocate, I have avoided the imputation of misrepresenting him. On the other hand, I have sacrificed the unity which a recasting would have assured, and have not supplied the accumulations of evidence, omitted through regard for the limits of a newspaper's space. Some of the authorities not cited are valuable, if not absolutely essential. A controversialist on paper, like a soldier on the field, likes to find himself thoroughly supported. It is specially pleasant to be helped from the other side.

Thus an admission by M. D. Conway, a man who discovers the traces of Oriental influences where few others can perceive them, has a peculiar interest. In replying to a criticism of his lecture on "Oriental Religions," which appeared in the *Cincinnati Gazette* of October 22, 1875, he explains his silence regarding the alleged parallelisms between Krishna and Christ by saying that he did not consider them " of much if any importance in comparative mythology." Even Mr. Graves in a moment of apparent forgetfulness, confesses that "the Vedas don't say a word about this god" (Krishna) which is a long step toward acknowledging what I have claimed.

It is also deserving of notice that Professor Whitney, of Yale College, who stands at the head of American Orientalists, and is eminent the world over, while holding Mr. Bentley's astronomical processes in no respect, agrees with his general results, and utterly repudiates the theories upon which Mr. Higgins has established his system of cycles and incarnations. He says that "the clear light of modern investigation has forever dispelled the wild dreams of men like Bailly, who could believe India to have been the primitive home of human knowledge and culture." He adds:

"It has been declared by Weber, the most competent of Indian scholars to pronounce upon such a point, and without contradiction from any quarter, that no mention even of the lesser planets, is to be found in Hindu literature until the modern epoch, after the influence of foreign astronomical science began to be felt. If, then, we find such a science making its sudden appearance in India at so late a period, we cannot help turning our eyes abroad to see whence it should have come. Nor can we long remain doubtful as to where it originated."

Having awarded Colebrooke the credit of first suggesting the idea, Professor Whitney shows that there are not only Western ideas but Greek words in the very centre and citadel of the Hindu science. Even the Surya Siddhanta, or Siddhanta of the Sun, revealed by that luminary to a demi-god, and ages ago handed down to man as an inestimable astronomical boon, purports in some manuscripts to have had the Romaka City, or Rome, for its place of "materialization." Professor Whitney coincides with Mr. Burgess, who shared with him the work of translating the famous treatise, in declaring the Surya markedly post-Christian, fixing on the date of 572 as most probable. He enforces his conclusions by solid arguments, for which we have no room. They may be found in detail in his paper on the Lunar Zodiac in the second series of his Oriental and Linguistic Studies.

Buddha has of late been an object of so much interest to thoughtful persons on account of the healthful look of many of his precepts, in spite of their wretched atheistical back-ground, that I ought, perhaps, to have considered his history more at length in my letters. I was writing for Mr. Graves, however, and so only aimed to controvert the claim that Buddha's supernatural birth was the prototype of that of Christ. This has been urged by others than my late opponent, as a support to the theory that the opening chapters of Matthew and the Buddhistic traditions are only different versions of the same legend. I may repeat, therefore, the statement that there is no positive proof of the exact correspondence of the existing Buddhistic writings with their alleged originals. Further, we know that there are two sets, the northern and southern, the one more extravagant than the other; and that those we have are often confessedly translations and revisions. Max Mueller argues indeed, the probability that many of the works, dating in their present form no further back than the fifth century of the Christian era, are faithful reproductions of the primitive versions or of those accepted as canonical at the great council, held about midway between the death of Buddha and the birth of Christ. This conclusion is not universally accepted, and is likely to be true only in part. Buddha's sayings may have been transmitted with only slight modification, but five hundred years afford ample time for the growth of personal legend.

Mr. Beale, translator of a curious life of Buddha from the Chinese, admits that all is dark and confused in Buddhistic chronology before the fifth Christian century. The Chinese work is itself a translation, and was made from a revised edition of its original—as Mr. Beale infers, two or three hundred years after the latter's first appearance, possibly before, possibly after the Christian era. This makes a pretty fragile and many-linked chain of guesswork rather than evidence. The book furnishes some curious coincidences, but many more glaring discrepancies between the story of Buddha and the gospel narrative. If Buddha, like Christ, was born of a virgin, his mother, Maia, died seven days after the birth of her child. She was transparent during her pregnancy; was a princess, not a maid in humble life. She lavished splendid gifts, and had been to a grand entertainment just previous to the journey during which she gave birth to a son, in a garden not in a stable. In the life of Buddha there is little that corresponds with that of Christ, except his going about and preaching. There is a closer parallel between his asceticism and that of John the Baptist.

He died a natural death, at an advanced age, while Christ was crucified before reaching thirty-five years.

When we compare the style of the Buddhistic narrative with that of the Evangelists, the contrast becomes still more marked. That of the former reminds one forcibly of the apocryphal gospels with Oriental embellishments. There is in more than one point, a near relationship of incident, and a decided affinity throughout. We know from the church fathers of the fourth century, who had heard of Buddha, and were not startled by any of the claims made for him, that Christianity had been diffused through India two centuries or more earlier. There is even reason for believing that it had very numerous professors all over the peninsula down to the fifth century. This was the very period when Buddhism had culminated there, only to be overpowered, a few centuries later by the Vishnuite sects; as the latter undeniably borrowed New Testament honors for Krishna, so the former would not be content that the Western missionaries should boast divine honors for their master which Buddha did not possess. If there were any appropriations, it is obvious that the Buddhists were the borrowers. There is nothing in pure Buddhism that requires a supernaturally born child. The Old Testament, on the contrary, whether regarded as inspired or not, contains predictions of the advent of such a being, and the Christian faith largely rests upon these prophecies. The supernatural forms the natural garb of the Jewish Messiah, while the phenomena of Buddha's birth hang round him like borrowed feathers, and such they undoubtedly are.

Were we even to admit, what cannot be proved, that traces of these legends are to be found in pre-Christian Buddhistic treatises, it would be more natural to suppose that the words of Isaiah had reached India—as they seem to have reached Persia—at this early date, than that the same specific ideas should have risen in two independent localities. This remark applies, of course, only to predictions of a supernatural birth, not to all the events accompanying it. I have shown the possibility of borrowing on the part of the Buddhists, the lack of evidence of any early native origins for their legends, and the improbability that Jewish Christians should go to India for conceptions which the sacred books of their own land supplied. The case appears plain, though it is the universal fashion of skeptics to make the Bible the debtor when there is any coincidence between its statements and the Ethnic traditions. Granting that it is merely a human composition, is its originality not entitled to the same presumption as that of writings, certainly its inferior in literary merit?

Thus much for Buddha; I should like to quote from Whitney additional testimony respecting the late origin of the Zend Avesta as we have it, but it would merely confirm what I have cited from Hardwick.

I have made it evident, as far as Mr. Graves and others of his school are concerned, that however gross and multiplied "pious frauds" may be, impious ones far exceed them in number and degree. When Robert Taylor, for example, professes to give all the historical corroborations of the New Testament, he artfully begins by quoting wild mediæval legends and fabrications, putting Tacitus and other early witnesses into the obscurest corner and discrediting them when he has placed them there. Such dishonesty recoils on the man who practices it. Mr. Graves is guilty of something of the same kind, though in a case of less importance, where he cites a religious paper's praise of "those so-called infidels," the early abolitionists, as an indorsement of the self-denial and virtues of skeptics generally.

These skeptical cavilers are so lynx-eyed also for flaws in the sacred history that they often fall into one pit while digging another. Thus M. Soury, a prominent French rationalist, while attempting to prove the story of Joseph in Egypt, to be largely a romance, in referring to the seizure of his coat by Potiphar's wife, thoughtlessly remarks that this was doubtless the one of many colors, which Jacob had given him. M. Soury forgot that the garment had been torn in pieces and dipped in blood by the brethren who sold its wearer into slavery. This stupidity of a man who professed to have studied Genesis from a highly philosophical standpoint, is amusingly exposed by his able reviewer Father Vigouroux. Mr. Graves has blundered as absurdly, and often less innocently, and the same is true of far abler champions of the destructive school. Their greatest mistake however, is their belief that they have made a clear path for themselves. Granting that they have overcome some difficulties, they have raised still more formidable ones.

Conceding that they have identified Christ with the heathen divinities—what then? The historical affiliations of the Old and New Testaments become unaccountable, and the total difference in the outcome of Christianity and its kindred systems is equally beyond explanation. I am writing for thoughtful men of ordinary acquirements, not for scholars, to whom my plainness and minuteness may seem unnecessary and tedious, and may therefore be excused for repeating what many have said before me, viz: That there is no one hypothesis which will account for all the data of the New Testament history, except that which assumes the credibility of its authors.

Neither myth nor tendency can overcome the testimony of the indisputably genuine Pauline epistles; enthusiasm and imposture are equally unsatisfactory, and a combination of any two or three of these, is like the mixing of an acid with an alkali. When the critics have done their best or worst to discredit the documents, there still remains, as Mill has said, the conception of the man Christ Jesus, the like of which could never have entered the imagination of Jew, Greek, or Roman.

J. T. P.

APPENDIX.

The notice taken by Mr. Graves of the following letters to the editor of the *Telegram* seems to justify their insertion here. The communication of Prof. Swing, deserves reproduction on its own merits.

A CARD FROM PROF. SWING.

To the Editor of the Richmond Telegram:

Your number of the 6th instant, contains such a long and careful analysis of Mr. Graves' book, entitled "The Sixteen Crucified Saviors," that I wish to thank not only the writer of such an article, but also the editor who, in these days of *"wicked editors,"* was willing to give so many columns to an essay indirectly upon the merits of the Founder of the Christian religion. The essay has so gratified my heart that I feel much like asking you to admit one word more into your paper; for speech causes more speech.

J. T. P. tempered his review with mercy, for after having shown that Mr. Graves had made up a poor collection of saviors, and might as well have assembled a hundred as to have found and labeled only sixteen, the gifted writer might have contended that if the man of Nazareth were the sixteenth of a group or the six hundredth, that would only show how anxious man every where has been, in all times, to find some one who could come able and willing to lead the heart up out of the vale of sorrow. The logical deduction from Mr. Graves' premises is not that Christ was a pretender, but that man will always seek a great deliverer so long as he may think that no adequate one has come. The "Sixteen Saviors" would be only sixteen forms which the longing to escape from sin and sorrow and death has assumed up to this date of human misfortune. Could Mr. Graves penetrate to the interior of Africa, he would find negro tribes looking back or forward to one of these mighty ones, and should he pass a summer with the Indians of Lake Superior, he would there learn that those children of the woods are expecting a chief to come who shall make the Indian return in triumph to displace the English and the French.

When Mr. Graves has found his score of "Saviors," he has not yet come anywhere near the conclusion he announces; but, on the opposite, he has only shown how the human family has always felt the need of some one who might become a connecting link between this life and a better one; but of the question whether man has found that link, or will soon find it, he does not so much as touch the outermost margin. It might be a pleasant task, or at least a long and interesting task, should Mr. Graves follow the Hebrew race alone, and mark how many deliverers that people thought they saw in the centuries after Isaiah, but if, after such a study, he should come to us with the conclusion that because of many errors in such vision, therefore, the Hebrews never at last gave birth to any divine leader, we should be compelled to assure him that he was guilty of a *non sequitur*. A child that has become separated from its mother in a London street will see that mother in a hundred women, now here and now there, and will run toward now this one and now that, with new assurance and new joy, but the cold looker-on must not, after witnessing a few mistakes of the child, come to us with the conclusion that the child had no mother in the outset. After the little crying one had blundered over "sixteen mothers," the question would remain untouched as to where the real parent might be concealed. "J. T. P." having made havoc of Mr. Graves's data, might thus make equal havoc of his conclusion.

The Christian confesses that the whole human race has been perfectly swept over by a perpetual wave of opinions and beliefs about a God; that in this tumult all shapes, moral and physical, of a Deity have been elaborated; but logic cannot deduce from these "Sixteen Gods," or sixteen million gods, the conclusion that the universe did not come from an intelligent Creator. In a similar manner the human race has been swept all over, in both space and time, by hopes and even visions of a deliverer; and, as out of many false images of a god, there came, at last, not atheism but a more true Father in Heaven. So up from a hundred dreams and embodiments of a Messiah, there may have come at last, and in

Bethlehem, a true Messenger from a higher realm. The book of Mr. Graves will show only how often human love and imagination will perceive a hero of liberty long before the real one comes; will find outlines of a Deity before they can give much of a definition of the Jehovah; and will show how an unhappy and mortal race passing in tears to a grave will often think it has found a friend and be often disappointed. But upon the question whether Jesus of Nazareth was, at last, this divine Friend, the volume contains no argument which need disturb for an instant the belief of the Christian. Yours, DAVID SWING.

Chicago, *Feb.* 10, 1879.

A CARD FROM HENRY WARD BEECHER.

To the Editor of the Richmond Telegram:

The paper containing your reply to several skeptical works came duly, and I read the matter with great interest, thinking all the while it ought to be published and circulated as a tract, or, thin book. It might, should that be done, be made a little fuller on some points, that men who have not seen the books replied to, might have the statements more fully set forth, before you reply.

I hope that Providence may direct you to a continuous work in this direction, for which you seem eminently fitted. I am, dear sir,

Very truly, yours,

HENRY WARD BEECHER.

Brooklyn, N. Y., *Feb.* 10, '79.

THE END.

TABLE OF CONTENTS.

		Page.
I.	INTRODUCTION—Infidelity among the masses..........	5
II.	LETTER TO MR. GRAVES—The Krishna legend post-Christian in its perfected form and in its coincidence with the Gospel Narrative—Hindoo astronomy recent and borrowed from abroad—Buddha historical, and not supernatural—The Zend Avesta—Mr. Graves's errors in mythology and philology..................	11
III.	MR. GRAVES'S REPLY and subsequent modifications and corrections,............................	55
IV.	REJOINDER TO MR. GRAVES.—The positions of the first letter reaffirmed—Fresh blunders of Mr. Graves in his defense exposed, and his discreditable treatment of the Bible set forth............................	105
V.	POSTSCRIPT—Additional confirmations of the letters—Appendix—Views of Prof. Swing and the Rev. Henry Ward Beecher............................	135

www.ingramcontent.com/pod-product-compliance
Lightning Source LLC
Chambersburg PA
CBHW022129160426

43197CB00009B/1201